About the Reviewers

Johnathan Iannotti is a software engineer and geek on an epic journey of life. His experience spans 15 years of technology solutions for start-ups, financial companies, healthcare, and military industries. He is passionate about web technology and has been creating hybrid apps since their inception. A full-stack developer by trade, he loves UX/UI, frontend development, and mobile.

He works for USAA, creating mobile applications for over 27,000 employees that serve their military membership. He is also a combat veteran, having served almost a decade in the United States Army.

Johnathan spends his time innovating, coding, and making the best of it all. When he's not plugged in, he spends as much time as he can with his beautiful wife and two children, who make it all possible.

You can follow Johnathan on Twitter at @notticode or visit his website, http://www.johnforhire.com/.

Yousuf Qureshi is an early adopter of technology and gadgets and has profound experience in the e-commerce, social media, analytics, and mobile apps sectors. He is a Cloudera Certified Developer for Apache Hadoop (CCDH).

His expertise includes development, technology turnaround, consulting, and architecture. He is also an experienced developer of Android, iOS, Blackberry, ASP. net MVC, Java, MapReduce, Distributed Search and Inverted Index algorithms, Hadoop, Hive, Apache Pig, Media API integration, and multiplatform applications.

Yousuf has also reviewed *jQuery Drag and Drop Grids How-To* and *Monitoring Hadoop* for Packt Publishing.

To my (late) grandparents, Abdullah Tanwar and Yasin Khokar.

Anthony Rumsey is a software developer at Adobe with a passion for creating well-designed and engaging user experiences. During his 15-year career, he has focused on the integration of web technologies into Adobe's enterprise software. More recently, his focus has shifted to exploring the capabilities of the mobile web and mobile apps, including contributions to the responsive simulator, touch interface, and PhoneGap integration in Adobe Experience Manager. Anthony happily resides in Ottawa, Canada, with his wife and two children.

Kasper Souren was born in the Netherlands and has been working with Internet technologies across the globe since 1998 for various companies and institutions, including CouchSurfing, Mercedes-Benz, Geekcorps Mali, the Dutch tax authorities, and the biggest Dutch social network. As of 2013, his favorite technology stack is Meteor with CoffeeScript. He's a cofounder of Hitchwiki.org, the ultimate resource for hitchhikers. You can visit his website at `http://guaka.org/` and also connect with him on Twitter at @guaka.

Tomasz Trejderowski is a middle-aged developer from Poland with hands-on experience in many programming languages and a wide range of IT aspects. He has been programming computers since the very first Commodore 64, which he received in his youth, and thus poses over 20 years of overall software development experience. You can access repositories and contributions on his GitHub profile and GitHub organizations that he is a part of at `https://github.com/trejder`.

He is a full-time PhoneGap and Yii2 developer and mobile market entrepreneur, constantly working on many innovative international start-ups and projects. You can visit his company website at `http://gaman.pl/` for more details.

Tomasz holds a PhD degree and has authored five books and over 40 articles (mostly in Polish). He is a happy husband of a wonderful wife and the father of two beautiful daughters.

www.PacktPub.com

Support files, eBooks, discount offers, and more

For support files and downloads related to your book, please visit www.PacktPub.com.

Did you know that Packt offers eBook versions of every book published, with PDF and ePub files available? You can upgrade to the eBook version at www.PacktPub.com and as a print book customer, you are entitled to a discount on the eBook copy. Get in touch with us at service@packtpub.com for more details.

At www.PacktPub.com, you can also read a collection of free technical articles, sign up for a range of free newsletters and receive exclusive discounts and offers on Packt books and eBooks.

https://www2.packtpub.com/books/subscription/packtlib

Do you need instant solutions to your IT questions? PacktLib is Packt's online digital book library. Here, you can search, access, and read Packt's entire library of books.

Why subscribe?

- Fully searchable across every book published by Packt
- Copy and paste, print, and bookmark content
- On demand and accessible via a web browser

Free access for Packt account holders

If you have an account with Packt at www.PacktPub.com, you can use this to access PacktLib today and view 9 entirely free books. Simply use your login credentials for immediate access.

Table of Contents

Preface

When you learn a new programming language, the traditional first step is to go through a *Hello, World* tutorial that teaches you everything you need to know to get a basic program working, such as one that prints the text *Hello, World* on the screen. In this sense, this book is the *Hello, World* tutorial to build your first PhoneGap application.

This book provides you with a great way to get started with PhoneGap and also gives detailed examples from the different areas that PhoneGap covers. It can be a great reference book for later use, in case you want to quickly refresh the essentials with PhoneGap. This book is updated with the latest releases so it supports the npm plugins too. It will take you through the process of installing everything that you need to get started with PhoneGap. It will cover the basics of PhoneGap, such as the command-line interface (CLI), PhoneGap plugins, and APIs provided by PhoneGap.

You'll find this book to be a great introduction to PhoneGap. It will give you a chance to learn some more about the Framework and give you the confidence to build something great that works across difference devices.

Enjoy the book!

What this book covers

Chapter 1, Get up and Running with PhoneGap, shows you what PhoneGap is used for, a basic understanding of what you can achieve with the framework, and why it is good to use.

Chapter 2, Mobile Platform Support, will go into more detail about the various platforms that are supported in PhoneGap and what their limitations are.

Chapter 3, Command-line Interface, shows you that the Cordova command line is crucial for the effective and streamlined development of PhoneGap applications. It will give you an overview of the capabilities and how to use them.

Chapter 4, Plugin Support, will show you that accessing any platform API is disabled by default, so all features are nicely packed in separate plugins that you can add and manage based on your needs.

Chapter 5, First PhoneGap Application, shows you how to create the first basic Hello World application with PhoneGap and tells you about the file structure organization and building a fully functional application.

Chapter 6, Accessing Native APIs, discusses the different hardware APIs that are available on most of the platforms PhoneGap supports.

Chapter 7, Accessing Media Content, covers additional native features that are available through JavaScript. This chapter will cover accessing the native camera capabilities and other media content on the device.

Chapter 8, Application Development Workflow, will cover the basics on how to work with the PhoneGap application development process and how to go through the phases until the application is built.

Online Chapter, Beyond PhoneGap – Ionic, goes a little bit forward by teaching you how to apply hybrid mobile UI that will work across different platforms and different screen sizes. Ionic framework seems like a great option to apply it on the top of the PhoneGap. This chapter can be found online at `https://www.packtpub.com/sites/default/files/downloads/Beyond_PhoneGap_Ionic.pdf`.

What you need for this book

In order to fully understand the concepts explained in the book, knowledge of the following subjects is mandatory:

- Knowledge of modern web application languages such as HTML5, CSS3, and JavaScript

- Being comfortable with the use of the Unix terminal and the Microsoft Windows command line

Who this book is for

The book is targeted at developers who want to develop hybrid mobile applications that have some basic understanding of frontend web development. It is intended for those developers who have experience with modern languages and development environments. Also, if you are familiar with the concepts of Object-oriented programming (OOP), reusable components, AJAX closures, and so on, this book will help you leverage that knowledge in the field of mobile development.

This book will cater to PhoneGap's users who want to know more about PhoneGap's broad range of capabilities and will also help you to expand the basic set of features using plugins.

Conventions

In this book, you will find a number of text styles that distinguish between different kinds of information. Here are some examples of these styles and an explanation of their meaning.

Code words in text, database table names, folder names, filenames, file extensions, pathnames, dummy URLs, user input, and Twitter handles are shown as follows: "Unzip the content into the folder `C:\Android\apache-ant-1.9.4`."

Any command-line input or output is written as follows:

```
phonegap create hello com.example.hello HelloWorld
cd hello
```

New terms and **important words** are shown in bold. Words that you see on the screen, for example, in menus or dialog boxes, appear in the text like this: "After opening the window, we should see an empty list. Switch to the **Device Definitions** tab and press **Create AVD**."

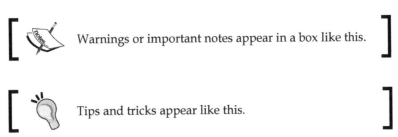

Warnings or important notes appear in a box like this.

Tips and tricks appear like this.

Reader feedback

Feedback from our readers is always welcome. Let us know what you think about this book—what you liked or disliked. Reader feedback is important for us as it helps us develop titles that you will really get the most out of.

To send us general feedback, simply e-mail feedback@packtpub.com, and mention the book's title in the subject of your message.

If there is a topic that you have expertise in and you are interested in either writing or contributing to a book, see our author guide at www.packtpub.com/authors.

Customer support

Now that you are the proud owner of a Packt book, we have a number of things to help you to get the most from your purchase.

Downloading the example code

You can download the example code files from your account at http://www.packtpub.com for all the Packt Publishing books you have purchased. If you purchased this book elsewhere, you can visit http://www.packtpub.com/support and register to have the files e-mailed directly to you.

Downloading the color images of this book

We also provide you with a PDF file that has color images of the screenshots/diagrams used in this book. The color images will help you better understand the changes in the output. You can download this file from https://www.packtpub.com/sites/default/files/downloads/4687OS_ColorImages.

Errata

Although we have taken every care to ensure the accuracy of our content, mistakes do happen. If you find a mistake in one of our books—maybe a mistake in the text or the code—we would be grateful if you could report this to us. By doing so, you can save other readers from frustration and help us improve subsequent versions of this book. If you find any errata, please report them by visiting http://www.packtpub.com/submit-errata, selecting your book, clicking on the **Errata Submission Form** link, and entering the details of your errata. Once your errata are verified, your submission will be accepted and the errata will be uploaded to our website or added to any list of existing errata under the Errata section of that title.

To view the previously submitted errata, go to https://www.packtpub.com/books/content/support and enter the name of the book in the search field. The required information will appear under the **Errata** section.

Piracy

Piracy of copyrighted material on the Internet is an ongoing problem across all media. At Packt, we take the protection of our copyright and licenses very seriously. If you come across any illegal copies of our works in any form on the Internet, please provide us with the location address or website name immediately so that we can pursue a remedy.

Please contact us at copyright@packtpub.com with a link to the suspected pirated material.

We appreciate your help in protecting our authors and our ability to bring you valuable content.

Questions

If you have a problem with any aspect of this book, you can contact us at questions@packtpub.com, and we will do our best to address the problem.

1
Get up and Running with PhoneGap

PhoneGap has brought a new paradigm to the field of mobile application development since its inception. It has tried to replace the old, fragmented mobile platform development, where each mobile device is developed using different programming languages and software patterns, with simple JavaScript and HTML.

Each new major version has managed to improve the performance and support features that were available only to native devices before. PhoneGap has come so far that most of the basic needs for a mobile application can be achieved with it, without writing a single line of code in the native language.

In this chapter, we will cover the following sections:

- A brief history
- What is PhoneGap?
- Setting up a local development environment

Let's get started with a quick introduction to PhoneGap.

A brief history

In 2007, Apple introduced its first smartphone: the iPhone. It changed the mobile phone industry forever. iPhone was the first smartphone that provided a browsing experience comparable to desktop web browsing. Many web pages were trying to mimic iPhone's look and feel for mobile use. Originally, iPhone didn't support third-party native apps. Many tried to create hybrid applications by hosting them on web servers. The application was running inside the Safari browser.

iPhone's immense success was noticed by competitors, especially Google. Google had planned to introduce Android before iPhone. Android back then was like Blackberry OS and interacted through the keyboard, but, seeing the success of iPhone, they decided to ditch the keyboard and open source it. Android had the ability to develop native applications. Apple allowed the development of native applications with the next version of iPhone. Competing platforms have different development stacks. It requires an extra amount of work to make them work on many popular platforms. This makes even the simplest application development across multiple platforms difficult. After some time, most platforms offered the ability to communicate between inline web browsers and the application's native code. With this, compiled hybrid applications became a reality. You could create the whole application with JavaScript, HTML, and CSS, and access native libraries through native code. It wasn't the best solution, since you needed to write native code that supports it, but that was going to change with the arrival of PhoneGap.

PhoneGap was started as a project at the iPhoneDevCamp event in 2008. It was started by a team of developers wanting to simplify cross-platform mobile development. Until then, it was easy to create applications for a single platform but there was no tool to manage it for multiple platforms. In the beginning, the idea was to create project templates that could be reused inside Xcode for iOS or Eclipse for Android to develop hybrid applications. Shortly afterwards, PhoneGap supported Blackberry OS. The team behind the project was from Nitobi Software company. They started to work on PhoneGap as a more serious tool for development. It began to be used for a full development cycle including preparing builds for deployment to the app stores or for using inside enterprises. PhoneGap won the People's Choice Award at O'Reilly Media's 2009 Web 2.0 Conference. Prior to Apple's developer license agreement version 4.0, the rules for submitting PhoneGap applications to the Apple app store were not clear and many apps were rejected for that reason. After updating the developer license agreement, Apple has confirmed that the framework has been approved for submitting PhoneGap applications.

In 2011, there were two important items of news for PhoneGap development. Adobe decided to acquire Nitobi Software as a part of the strategy for moving away from Adobe Flash on mobile devices. The other news was that they were going to open source PhoneGap and contribute it to the Apache Foundation. Since being contributed to the Apache Foundation, it changed to Apache Callback, Apache DeviceReady, and finally Apache Cordova (`http://cordova.apache.org`). After Adobe acquired it, the team behind PhoneGap worked full time on the project and the updates are being delivered on a monthly basis.

The PhoneGap brand has been preserved by Adobe. PhoneGap is now a fork of Apache Cordova with some extra features. PhoneGap and Cordova were basically identical until the release of version 2.*x*. After that, the development went into simplifying project creation. A command-line interface was created for most common actions, and the core features were separated into numerous plugins. The new process simplified the creation and installation of new plugins.

What is PhoneGap?

In short, PhoneGap (http://www.phonegap.com/) is a distribution of Cordova. Cordova is an open source mobile framework that gives an alternative to native development and the existing application is reusable on other platforms with little or no modification to the code.

To be more precise, PhoneGap is an application framework that is capable of developing, and later building, native applications that can be deployed across different mobile platforms, thus simplifying the process and saving a lot of time. PhoneGap gives you the ability to use a single programming language—JavaScript together with HTML and CSS—to build the user interface.

With PhoneGap, any web developer can start developing mobile applications with no need to learn additional skills, apart from learning about PhoneGap's command-line interface (CLI) commands and PhoneGap's API. In a matter of hours, you can create a working prototype that can be tested directly on the user's smartphone, or built and deployed to the app store as a normal native application in all major application stores (iTunes app store, Android Apps on Google Play, Amazon Appstore, and Windows Store).

PhoneGap can be used to target support for multiple platforms from day one without needing to have another developer for another technology stack. Currently it supports the following major platforms:

- Apple iOS (https://developer.apple.com/devcenter/ios/index.action)
- Google Android (http://developer.android.com/index.html)
- Microsoft Windows Phone (http://msdn.microsoft.com)
- Blackberry 10 (https://developer.blackberry.com/)
- Firefox OS (https://developer.mozilla.org/en-US/docs/Mozilla/Firefox_OS)
- Tizen (https://developer.tizen.org)

PhoneGap's basic philosophy is to use the feature of the operating system that enables communication with the native code directly from the JavaScript inside the device's web browser, which is also being used as a UI rendering engine. There is no defined standard for UI rendering, so it can be developed to look like a regular page since we are defining the whole UI interface with HTML and CSS; or we can use available solutions that were specially built for the size of the screen on mobile devices.

Where can it be used?

As PhoneGap is already a stable framework and is constantly evolving, there are a lot of features that were previously available only for native applications but that can be used now inside PhoneGap. Let's list some of the major features that are being supported by the latest PhoneGap version:

- Camera
- Capture photos
- Compass
- Connection status
- Contact list
- Device details
- Events sent from the native environment
- File management
- Geolocation
- Multi-language support and localization
- In AppBrowser, the ability to run another browser view inside the PhoneGap application
- Media
- Storage

Most of these features are available through calling native methods, but as HTML5 is progressing, many of these features are available through native web view HTML5 method calls, thus removing dependency on the native code. If you want to see what features are supported with HTML5, you can take a look at this page (http://html5please.com/). It shows support for the various mobile browsers.

What PhoneGap is not

It is not a solution that fits all needs. It depends on the features and utility of the application, which can determine if PhoneGap is fit for its needs. If you are looking to develop a graphic-intensive 3D game or application that needs to use all the processing power the device has, then probably it is not the best choice to start with. PhoneGap can easily be used for all applications that do not involve a lot of animations or complicated transitions that are not easily achieved inside the HTML and CSS environment.

There is another misconception: many developers think that PhoneGap compiles JavaScript code into native binary code, which is not true; it only packages the JavaScript, HTML, and CSS into a wrapper that runs the content inside a sandboxed web page.

Competition

There are a lot of alternatives with differing perspectives, ranging from using the web page shortcut on the home screen as an icon, to emulating the application feel, running a regular web page like an application or even building the JavaScript source code to a real native application.

Here we will take a look at four different solutions that all have advantages and disadvantages:

- **jQuery Mobile** (http://jquerymobile.com/)

Advantages	Disadvantages
Popular as a mobile page	Could be too heavy for some smartphones
A lot of plugin support	No official paid support
Based on jQuery	
Great tools, such as Theme Roller and Codiqa UI builder	
It is used only as the visual part of the application; it can be used with multiple JavaScript frameworks	

- **Sencha Touch** (http://www.sencha.com/products/touch/)

Advantages	Disadvantages
Based on ExtJS	Sometimes slow (client-side DOM generation)
Full MVC framework	No native controls
Official paid support	Few customization options
Sencha Architect	Performance

- **Titanium** (http://www.appcelerator.com/titanium/)

Advantages	Disadvantages
Rapid prototyping	Increased complexity and costs
Native UI	Flexibility limitations
Web oriented	Native UI can be limiting sometimes
Cross-platform support	

- **PhoneGap** (http://www.phonegap.com)

Advantages	Disadvantages
Single code base for all platforms	PhoneGap can be a complex framework if not understood well, thus making it less responsive
Rapid deployment	No default UI
Access to native functions	Limited access to more advanced features without additional plugins
Offline usage	Complex business logic

PhoneGap or Cordova?

It seems that there is a lot of confusion between these two because they share the same history and their paths diverged only recently. From the beginning the project was called PhoneGap, but once Adobe bought the company behind it, it decided to open source the majority of the code while keeping the name for its use and giving a new name (Cordova) to the open source project.

Since then, PhoneGap has been built on top of the Cordova project with some additional libraries and tighter integration with other PhoneGap tools and services; the most prominent for PhoneGap developers is PhoneGap Build, which we will go into in greater detail in the next chapter.

There is not much difference for the beginner between PhoneGap and Cordova, apart from the ability to build native applications for all major platforms from any operating system with the help of PhoneGap Build. This makes it more useful in some cases since the majority of people do not like switching from their favorite operating system.

Setting up a local development environment

Since this book covers all major operating system platforms, before we start to learn more about PhoneGap and its useful features we need to prepare the development environment. The PhoneGap website (http://phonegap.com/install/) has instructions on how to install it, which should be fairly easy to achieve. However, in reality, each platform requires us to install additional libraries and simulators to be able to run them for different mobile platforms.

There are two ways to develop PhoneGap applications. Until PhoneGap introduced the **command-line interface (CLI)**, the only way was to develop plugins for the **integrated development environment (IDE)**, such as Xcode or Eclipse. With the introduction of the CLI, it was possible to develop PhoneGap mobile applications with PhoneGap SDK inside your favorite text editor or integrated developer environment. In this book, we are going to use the latter option; since most developers have different opinions about editors, it is better to stay neutral on this topic.

However, for this book I will be using Sublime Text 3 (http://www.sublimetext.com/3), a plain text editor that is one of the most popular choices nowadays and has numerous plugins and extensions to work with. Since it supports Windows, Mac OS, and Linux, it won't be included in the installation process for a specific operating system. On the provided link, you can download the text editor and install it with the provided information. Sublime Text 3 can be used for free for as long as you like (you will be prompted to buy it from time to time); this is a fully working editor without any limits. But I would strongly advise you to get the full version and support the people behind it since they have done a great job and it only costs $70 and doesn't have restrictions on the number of machines for a single user.

There is a great free alternative to Sublime Text called Atom editor, which is open source and available at the following page: https://atom.io/. It will be sufficient to do the work but it doesn't come with lot of plugins like Sublime Text.

In the following pages, there will be instructions on how to cover the installation process for the three most popular operating systems that developers are using: Windows, Mac OS, and Ubuntu. For other Linux distributions, it should not be too hard to adapt the Ubuntu installation process, especially if you are using Debian. Let us get started.

Mac OS

In the beginning, PhoneGap started as a way to create iOS applications with JavaScript and HTML to create a fully functional iOS application without writing a single line of code in Objective-C. To get started for Mac OS, there are few more steps than the instructions on the PhoneGap website (`http://phonegap.com/install/`) are telling us to perform. We will need to install simulators for supported mobile devices. On this platform, we will install support for iOS and Android development. For installation purposes, it is assumed that this is being installed as a clean installation so, if you already have some of the libraries installed, it is advisable to update them to the latest version to make sure they are working properly. For Mac OS, the latest operating system version (Yosemite) will be used.

The easiest way to install the various Unix tools and open source software onto Mac OS X is via a package manager but unfortunately OS X does not come with one; however, there are some alternatives that we can use instead. We are going to use Homebrew (`http://brew.sh/`).

If you already have your own package manager preference or you want to compile it from the source code, you are encouraged to use the latest version for the library.

Before installing Homebrew, we need to install Xcode (`https://itunes.apple.com/au/app/xcode/id497799835?mt=12`) so we can build and run applications in the iOS simulator:

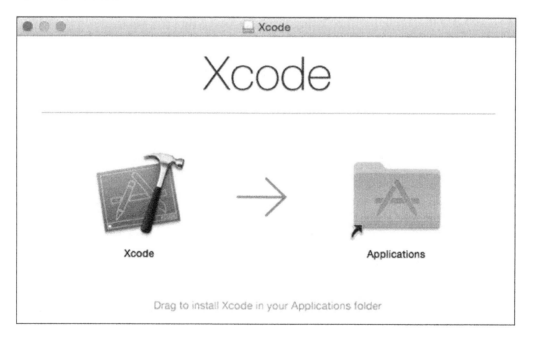

To install the Xcode component, perform the following steps:

1. Download the image and then drag the `Xcode` icon into the `Applications` folder. Before proceeding with the next step, you need to open Xcode and agree to the license, as it needs to install additional components:

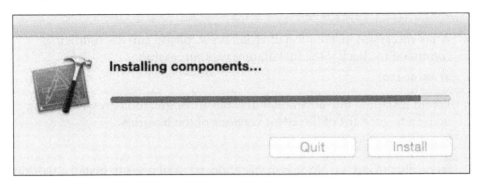

2. After the components are installed, you need to install the Xcode command line tools with the following command:

    ```
    xcode-select —install
    ```

3. This will open the following prompt to install the required tools. Select **Install** to install the required libraries, and wait until everything is successfully installed:

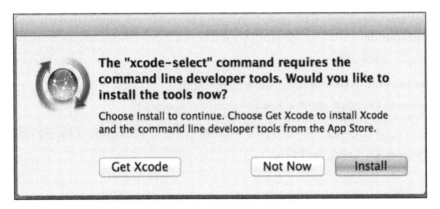

4. To download and install Homebrew, run the following installation script on the command line. It will ask you for a few details before proceeding, but you can leave the default values in use, unless you have a specific reason to change them, then wait for the script to finish:

```
ruby -e "$(curl -fsSL https://raw.githubusercontent.com/Homebrew/
install/master/install)"
```

5. After successful installation of Homebrew, please run the following command to check if the installation was successful:

```
brew doctor
```

6. Before installing any additional libraries through Homebrew, let us run update to get a list of the latest versions of the libraries:

```
brew update
```

7. Since PhoneGap is a Node.js application, we will need to install a working version of Node.js. With Homebrew, the process of installing additional libraries is easy; just run the following command:

```
brew install node
```

8. To be able to build and run applications in the Android simulator, you need to install the full Android **software development kit (SDK)** by running the following command:

```
brew install android-sdk
```

9. Add the Android SDK path to be used with PhoneGap with the following commands:

```
vi ~/.bash_profile
```

10. At the end of the file, add the following line:

```
export ANDROID_HOME=`brew --prefix android`
```

11. Save and close the file and run the following to reload the newest updates:

```
source ~/.bash_profile
```

12. The following command will launch the Android SDK manager window and you should see the recommended libraries already preselected:

```
android sdk
```

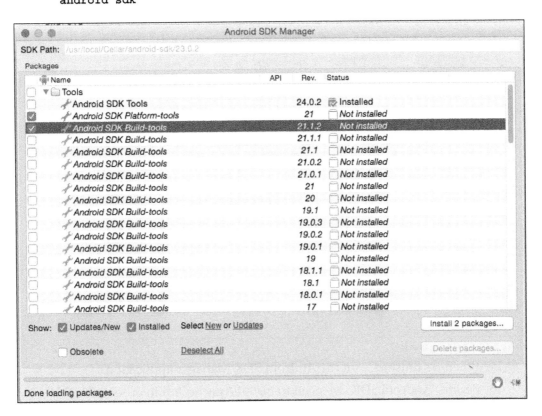

13. Click the **Install 2 packages** button and accept all the agreements for the required libraries. Then press the **Install** button:

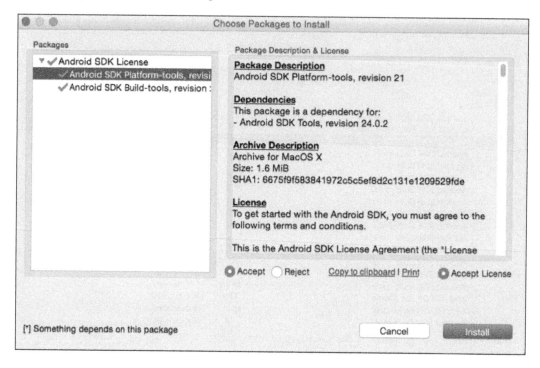

14. When it's finished, quit the Android SDK Manager application.

15. Besides Android SDK, we need to install Apache Ant in order to be able to build and run the applications inside Android Simulator. Run the following command:

    ```
    brew install ant
    ```

16. In order to emulate an Android device, we need to first create a virtual device. Run the following command to set up the default Android virtual device:

    ```
    android avd
    ```

17. This will launch the Android Virtual Device Manager. Click the **Device Definitions** tab and select a sample device. From the list select the **Nexus 5** profile, and press the **Create AVD** button as shown in the following screenshot:

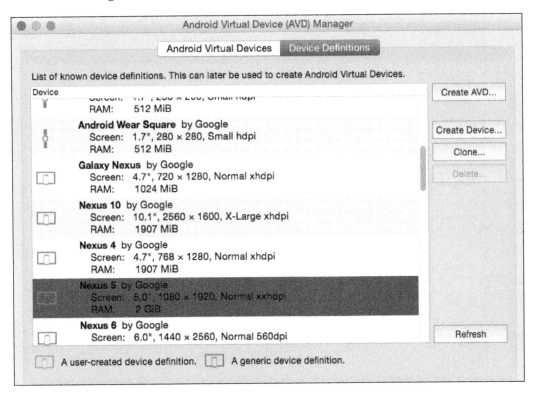

18. Fill out the device profile and click **OK**:

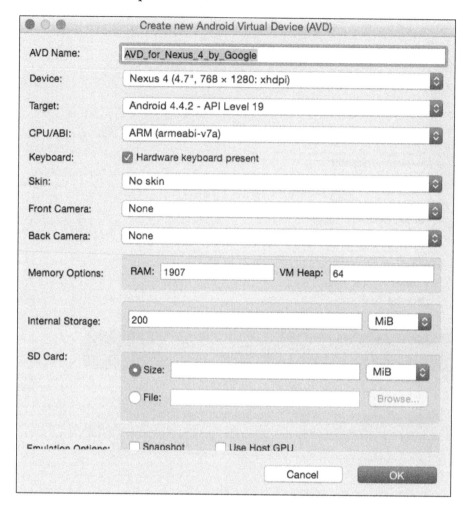

19. Close the Android Virtual Device Manager window.

20. Next we need to install the required libraries (to be able to build and run applications in the iOS simulator) by installing the Node.js library to control the iOS simulator directly from the command line:

```
sudo npm install -g ios-sim
```

21. When all the required libraries and tools are installed, install PhoneGap with the following command:

```
sudo npm install -g PhoneGap
```

22. To verify we can build and launch applications in both simulators, let us create and run a quick sample application by running the following command:

```
PhoneGap create hello com.example.hello HelloWorld
cd hello
```

23. This creates a basic sample application. Next we need to verify it works on the Android and iOS simulator.

24. For iOS we need to open the iOS simulator and run the application. Run the following command:

```
phonegap run ios --emulator
```

25. To test if everything is working well on Android, we are going to run the following command, which should run Android Device Simulator as we selected before:

```
phonegap run android —emulator
```

Linux

Linux is well known for having multiple distributions that have different ways of installing new libraries on it. For this book, we are going to use one of the most popular distributions: Ubuntu. Ubuntu is built on top of Debian so installing on both of them shouldn't be much different. As for the other distributions, it shouldn't be too hard to adapt the following commands for these environments. Perform the following steps:

1. First we need to fully update Ubuntu to avoid any issues while installing the required libraries:

   ```
   sudo apt-get update
   sudo apt-get install build-essential
   ```

2. Next we install some libraries that are required to finish the installation:

   ```
   sudo apt-get install python-software-properties python g++ make
   ```

3. Since PhoneGap is a Node.js application, we will need to install the latest working version of Node.js. Make sure you install Node.js and not node, which is a different library:

   ```
   sudo apt-get install nodejs
   ```

4. While that's all you need to do to install Node.js, there is a small detail that you need to take care of. When Ubuntu installs the package, it names the Node.js executable nodejs. The problem is that many applications, including PhoneGap, expect the executable to be named node. To fix this inconsistency, simply create a symlink named node that points to Node.js as follows:

   ```
   sudo ln -s /usr/bin/nodejs /usr/bin/node
   ```

5. Next we need to install additional libraries for Node.js:

   ```
   sudo apt-get install npm
   ```

6. Finally, we can install the PhoneGap library by running the following command:

   ```
   sudo npm install -g phonegap
   ```

7. Now we need to install the Ant tool, required to build and run Android applications:

   ```
   sudo apt-get install ant
   ```

8. Since Android uses the Java language, we will need to install Java JRE and Java JDK, which supports it:

```
sudo apt-get install openjdk-7-jre
sudo apt-get install openjdk-7-jdk
```

9. Now it is time to install the actual Android SDK. Run the following command:

```
wget http://dl.google.com/android/android-sdk_r24.0.2-linux.tgz
tar zxvf android-sdk_r24.0.2-linux.tgz
```

10. Let us move the content of the Android SDKs to a more appropriate location:

```
sudo mv android-sdk-linux/ /opt/android/
```

11. Now we need to set up paths to be executable from anywhere inside the terminal. Let us open the vi editor:

```
vi ~/.bashrc
```

12. Enter the following lines at the end of the file:

```
export ANDROID_HOME="/usr/local/android-sdk-linux/tools"
export ANDROID_PLATFORM_TOOLS="/usr/local/android-sdk-linux/platform-tools"
export PATH="$PATH:$ANDROID_HOME:$ANDROID_PLATFORM_TOOLS"
```

13. To use the command in the same terminal, you need to run the following command:

```
source ~/.bashrc
```

14. Now that we have set up the Android SDK environment, we need to run the configuration application to download the required libraries and emulators. Run the following command:

```
android
```

15. Execute Android from the shell. This is a good first test to make sure you've done everything right up to now. If you get an error, rerun through the preceding steps and make sure that you've installed all the requirements and added your environment variables correctly.

If there is no error, you should see that executing Android opens up a kind of package manager that you can use to install different Android components. By default, a certain number of these will be pre-selected for installation. Leave them as is and, in addition, tick the box next to the entry named **API 4.4.2 (API 19)**. Once you've done that, download and install everything by accepting the license, as shown in the following screenshot:

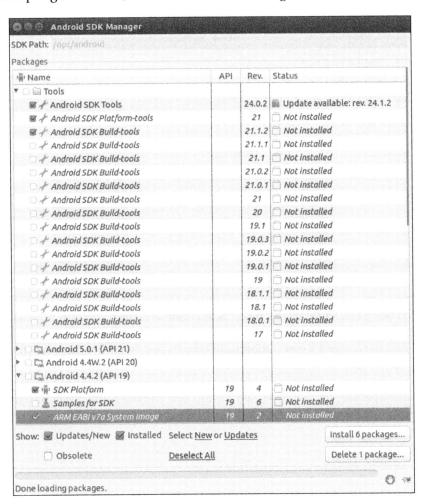

16. Next we need to confirm installation of the requested packages, by clicking on **Install**:

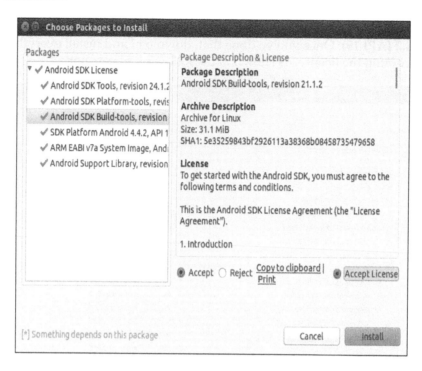

17. The last step before trying it out is to create an Android emulator that will emulate a working Android device on your computer. By default no emulator is set, so we need to set it manually by running the following command:

```
android avd
```

18. After opening the window, we should see an empty list. Switch to the **Device Definitions** tab and press **Create AVD**:

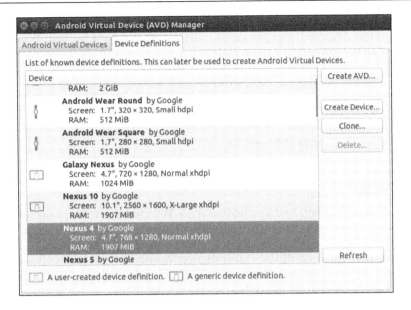

19. For our emulator, we will use the following settings:

20. After we have installed all the required libraries and the emulator required to run the Android app, we can finally create our first test application by running the following command:

```
phonegap create hello com.example.hello HelloWorld
cd hello
```

21. To verify everything is working fine, you need to run the emulator:

```
phonegap run android —emulator
```

Windows

If you want to develop and test applications for Windows phones, you will need to have a working Windows computer to hand because you can only run them there.

There are multiple versions of the Windows operating system but it should be fairly easy to use any of them by carrying out the following instructions, since most of the libraries and applications are available as an installer. Thus, you can simply go ahead with the installation process and the only thing you need to do manually is to set the environment variables to be reachable from any command prompt.

The easiest way is to create a Development directory in your home directory (C:\ Users\yourusername\Development). For ease, you might want to drag that folder into the Favorites list in Explorer, too. We will add all the source code we work on to the examples there.

Let us start with the stable Java SE Development Kit. Perform the following steps:

1. Download the latest available version that works on your computer from http://www.oracle.com/technetwork/java/javase/downloads/index.html.

2. Run the downloaded file and go through the following steps:

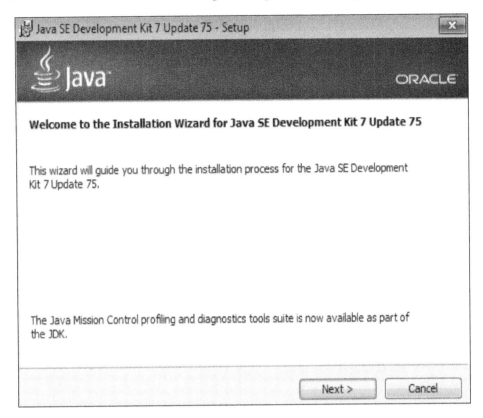

3. You need to make sure that you have the following paths set in your Advanced System Properties Environment Variables.

4. You need to set the path to be visible so it can be run as a command from the command prompt. Navigate to **Control Panel | System and Security | System**. There you need to click on the **Advanced** tab, as shown in the following screenshot:

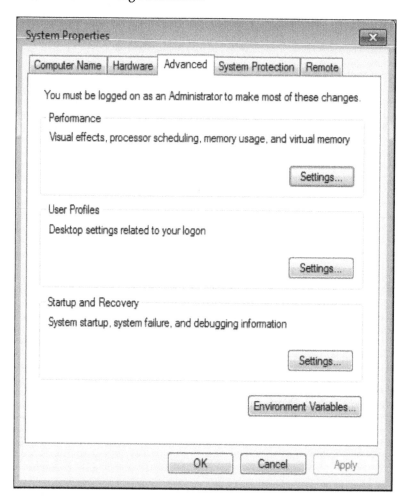

You will need to press the **Environment Variables** button and update system variables with the following data:

1. Create a new system variable:

   JAVA_HOME with value: C:\Program Files\Java\jdk1.7.0_75

2. Next we need to edit an existing variable:

   Path and add the following value ;%JAVA_HOME%\bin

3. Add the preceding line at the end of the remaining paths and make sure it is preceded by a ; (semicolon). It is important not to forget it:

4. You can test it by running the following command:

   ```
   java
   ```

5. In the command prompt, if you see the regular Java help text printout response then the Java environment is all set. Close the command prompt.

6. Next we need to download Android SDK for Windows, which is available as an automated installer. Download the latest SDK version from: `https://developer.android.com/sdk/index.html`.

7. Make sure you do not use the default proposed folder since you might have some problems with accessing folder content in the following steps. Instead, set the installation location to `C:\Android\android-sdk`.

8. We now need to go back to add an additional environment variable in the Android SDK location as we did before for Java SDK.

9. First we add a new system variable:

   `ANDROID_HOME` with value `C:\Android\android-sdk`

10. Next we need to edit the existing variable:

    `Path` and append additional value `;%ANDROID_HOME%\platform-tools;%ANDROID_HOME%\tools`

11. Again, do not forget to add a `;` (semicolon) at the beginning.

12. Next we need to open another command prompt to check whether it is installed properly. Run the following command:

    android

13. This will open the Android SDK Manager, where we will need to select which Android version to download; this is going to be used inside the emulator:

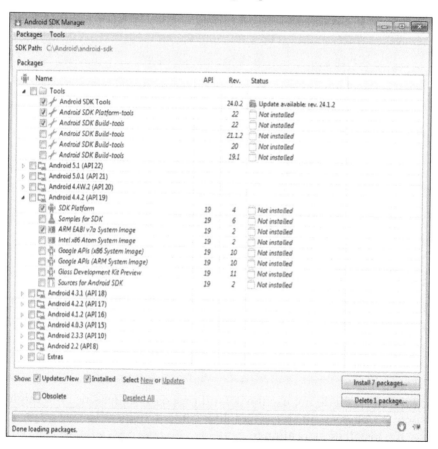

14. After selecting the packages ticked in the screenshot, you need to click **Install 7 packages** and wait until they are installed.

We need to install the `git` command (used for many libraries) and later plugins that we will require to make it work with PhoneGap. Perform the following steps:

1. Download and install the git installer from `http://git-scm.com/download/win`.

2. You should open the installer, follow the instructions, and select the predefined values. After installation, repeat the same process with system variables and add the variable `GIT_HOME` with a value `C:\Program Files\git`. Add additional information to the existing `PATH` by appending: `;%GIT_HOME%\bin`.

3. Again, to test whether it is working, run the `git` command in the newly opened command prompt.

4. Ant is a tool that is required by Android to build all the code into the Android application package. You need to download and install Ant from: `http://www.us.apache.org/dist/ant/binaries/`. Select the latest version that has the .zip extension.

5. Unzip the content into the folder `C:\Android\apache-ant-1.9.4`.

6. Again set the system variables with the creation of a new variable `ANT_HOME` with the value `C:\Android\apache-ant-1.9.4`. Update the existing `Path` variable `PATH` by appending `;%ANT_HOME%\bin`.

7. In the next step, we will install the latest version of Node.js from the `http://nodejs.org` as an installer. After it is downloaded, run the downloaded file, which will guide you through the process. The Installer should set all the path variables you need to run it. To confirm the installation worked, run the `node` command in the command prompt. It will open the node console, which you can close by pressing *Ctrl + C* twice.

8. The last step is to install the PhoneGap library by running the following command at the command prompt:

```
npm install -g phonegap
```

9. To verify we have installed PhoneGap properly, we simply run the `phonegap` command at the command prompt; this should return details about PhoneGap.

10. There is one last thing we need to do before running the test project. We need to create Android Emulator Start by running the following command:

```
android avd
```

11. By default, there are no emulators, so we need to create one before starting. Press **Create...** which will open a window to create a new emulator. Enter the following settings and press **OK**:

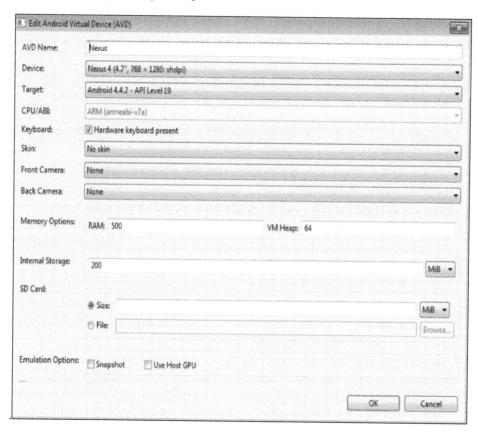

12. A new emulator should be listed. Close the application.

13. To verify we can build and launch the application in the simulator, let us create and run a quick sample application by running the following command:

```
phonegap create hello com.example.hello HelloWorld
cd hello
```

14. This creates a basic sample application, so next we need to run it to verify it works on the Android simulator.

15. To test that everything is working well, we are going to run the following command that should run Android Device Simulator, as selected before:

```
phonegap run android —emulator
```

16. You should see it running an example.

Summary

In this introductory chapter we covered a lot. We got a quick overview of what, as a framework, PhoneGap is and is not. Before we start to do any real work with PhoneGap, we need to have installed all the required tools that we covered in this chapter in detail, for all three major platforms.

After finishing this chapter, you should have a fully functional setup to start developing PhoneGap applications on your favorite operating system.

In the next chapter, we will cover the support for different platforms and the features that each platform supports. We will come to understand what PhoneGap Build is and how to test usability on native devices.

2
Mobile Platform Support

A major key to development in a framework that supports hybrid applications lies in the ability to provide access to as many as possible mobile platforms. In this area, PhoneGap has managed to keep the pace and add new platforms as they achieve significant market penetration. In this chapter, we will go over the platforms that are currently supported and the features that are available to a specific platform. In this chapter we are covering the essential topics related to mobile platform support:

- Supported platforms
- PhoneGap Build
- The PhoneGap Developer App

Supported platforms

As the PhoneGap platform has been evolving, the number of supported platforms has been rising all the time. Some platforms were dropped due to the loss of popularity and new ones were added to it. The following page shows the updates for platform support: http://docs.PhoneGap.com/en/4.0.0/guide_support_index.md.html#Platform%20Support.

The following platforms are supported in the latest version of PhoneGap:

- Amazon Fire OS
- Android
- BlackBerry 10
- Firefox OS
- iOS
- Ubuntu Touch
- Windows Phone 8

- Windows Phone 8.1
- Tizen OS

However, not all the platforms support the available plugins and features that they provide. It depends a lot on the type of the platform and feature that is supported by the device. As it started with iOS, it has the best coverage of all the basic features, and extended features as well through plugins. The second most supported platform is Android as the other platforms are not represented in all the plugins because it is usually required to create some native code to be able to run the code.

In the latest version of PhoneGap, the gap between the features of native and hybrid applications has narrowed a lot as most of the features that you usually need for your application have been ported through plugins in order to support them. A native application is an application particular to a given mobile platform that is usually written in a specific language that OS endorses (Objective-C or Swift for iOS and Java for Android). A hybrid application makes it possible to embed the HTML5 application inside the native container. It can be added to the app store and it runs as a native application, though it is running the whole application inside WebView. If you are looking to develop an application that requires intensive processing power or use some high quality graphics, then probably a hybrid solution is not there as yet to support this kind of request and it is usually better to develop it as a native application.

Supported features by platform

In the following section, we will explore the varying feature support based on the platforms that we use. In general, major platforms support them. The following are some of the features:

- Accelerometer: Supported on all platforms
- Battery Status: Supported on all platforms except Ubuntu Touch
- Camera: Supported on all platforms
- Compass: Supported on all platforms except Firefox OS
- Connection Type: Supported on all platforms except Firefox OS
- Contacts: Supported on all platforms except Firefox OS
- Device Information: Supported on all platforms
- File management: Supported on all platforms except Firefox OS and Tizen OS
- File Transfer: Supported on all platforms except Firefox OS and Tizen OS
- Geolocation: Supported on all platforms
- Globalization: Supported on all platforms

- InApp Browser: Supported on all platforms except Firefox OS and Tizen OS, and partial support for Windows 8.1

- Media Access: Supported on all platforms except Firefox OS

- Notifications: Supported on all platforms except Firefox OS

- Storage Database: Supported on all platforms except Firefox OS

- Vibration: Supported on all platforms except Ubuntu Touch, Tizen OS, and Windows 8.1

Support for development

Though PhoneGap tries to support all the available platforms, there are limitations imposed by the owners of the platform that limits the platforms to selected operating systems. This in turn limits the development process to multiple operating systems, which we can overcome with the help of PhoneGap Build. We will get to know more about this in the next chapter.

Not all operating systems have the same support for developing for all mobile platforms. Let's see what different operating systems support:

- Mac OS supports the development of the Amazon FireOS, Android, Blackberry 10, Firefox OS, and iOS platforms

- Windows supports the development of the Amazon FireOS, Android, Blackberry 10, Firefox OS, and Windows Phone platforms

- Linux supports the development of the Amazon FireOS, Android, Blackberry 10, Firefox OS, and Ubuntu Touch (limited only to Ubuntu distribution) platforms

As we can see, the most common mobile platform is the most represented among all the operating systems; thus we will focus all the development in this book on it. Android will be the easiest to work with as most of the code that supports the plugins that we will be using can be transferred to some of the other platforms.

PhoneGap Build

There are a lot of questions about the difference between PhoneGap and Cordova, and PhoneGap Build is usually the answer. PhoneGap has the built-in support for managing PhoneGap Build directly from the command-line interface while Cordova doesn't. Until the introduction of the command-line interface, building an application for multiple platforms required you to run different development environments at the same time. This has changed a lot with the introduction of the PhoneGap Build in 2012.

PhoneGap Build is a cloud-based answer to the issue of building applications for the various platforms that are not supported on the operating system you use. PhoneGap Build can be used as a cloud compiler that generates applications for every supported platform, though the support for all PhoneGap platforms is limited. In the latest version, it supports only three major platforms: iOS, Android, and Windows.

PhoneGap Build makes it very simple for you to develop applications. You can test them in the web browser, upload the code, and run the build process for all the available platforms on PhoneGap Build. It saves time as everything is happening in the cloud concurrently. This makes the process of development much easier unless you are not using the feature that is specific to that particular platform or device, and the feature that we need for our application to function cannot be simulated in the browser.

Android is the only mobile platform that has support for all the major platforms. Therefore, this makes Android the perfect platform to develop on a machine of your personal preference, as it works with anything that you already use.

One great advantage of PhoneGap Build is that you can build mobile apps without even installing anything on your local computer. You just need to open your favorite editor, test the app in the browser, and use PhoneGap Build to build it. However, this applies only to those applications that do not need access to hardware sensors. The introduction of the command-line interface (CLI) greatly reduced the need for PhoneGap Build as you can build applications for multiple platforms with a single line. A big disadvantage is that the less popular mobile platforms lacked support and it seems that they are going to be removed entirely from service in the future, except the top three platforms. Another major drawback is the fact that, in order to use PhoneGap Build for serious work, you need to pay for it.

Platform support

The support for the platforms varies over time. Currently, PhoneGap Build supports the building of applications in the following three major platforms only:

- iOS
- Android
- Windows Phone

After PhoneGap 3.0, PhoneGap Build has dropped the support for the following platforms: Blackberry, Symbian, and WebOS.

Using PhoneGap Build

Visit `https://build.PhoneGap.com` and go through the registration process. This will help you to create an Adobe account that is usable with the other services that Adobe provides or you can reuse the existing one.

When you click on the following link, you should land on the homepage where you can read more about PhoneGap Build:

For this chapter, you can select the free version, which is limited to a single application submission. If you like the tool, you will need to invest money in the subscription. There is one exception: you can build as many open source projects as you want, for free, as long as they are hosted on GitHub. After you select the plan, you will be presented with the following interface to choose the project that you want to add. You can submit application's source code directly from GitHub if you are using it for the code versioning. You can also upload the zipped file of the whole project that we created previously. The uploading of zipped files is not available for open source projects; you can use only GitHub for this.

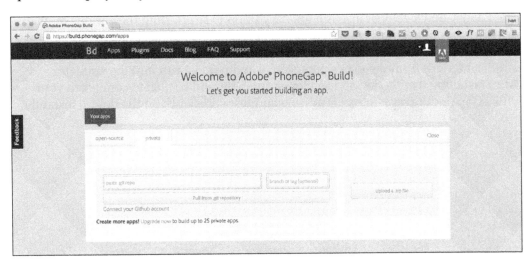

There are some limitations in case you don't have the developer keys for the supported platform. iOS is the least forgiving among them as you need to have a developer account to be able to build the installable package for it. You will need to provide a developer key for each platform if you want to submit it on their app store.

The following screenshot will show you the default page for your application:

The PhoneGap Developer App

The PhoneGap Developer app is a great addition to supporting the various mobile devices without needing to build and install separate versions into the various devices. It provides a simple testing utility for developers who want to check out the interface from the user's perspective and not just run it in the emulator. After installing the PhoneGap Developer app, you will be able to connect to your PhoneGap desktop app in order to view and test your work on the device instantly.

You can read more about it at `http://app.PhoneGap.com`.

Currently, the PhoneGap Developer app is being supported on all the three major platforms. The URLs to the app stores for each platform are as follows:

- iOS application: `https://itunes.apple.com/app/id843536693`
- Android application: `https://play.google.com/store/apps/details?id=com.adobe.PhoneGap.app`
- Windows application: `http://www.windowsphone.com/en-us/store/app/PhoneGap-developer/5c6a2d1e-4fad-4bf8-aaf7-71380cc84fe3`

How to use it

To show you how to use the PhoneGap Developer app, we can reuse the previous hello project or run a command to create a new project:

```
phonegap create developerApp
cd developerApp
phonegap serve
```

After you run the last command, you will see a local network web address that you will need to enter in the PhoneGap app that you previously installed in your smartphone. You will see the following screen if you use the iOS application, however, all supported devices will have the same interface once you run it in your device, which means the application works the same on all the platforms. For this example, note that there might be network limitations between your computer and the mobile device. Both the computer and mobile device must be connected to the same local network in order to make this work.

Summary

This chapter was an overview of the supported platforms in PhoneGap along with the features that each platform supports. As one of the most supported platforms is Android, we will be using it for the following examples in this book. Next, we took a quick look at PhoneGap Build, which is one of the main differences between PhoneGap and Cordova. In the end, we got to know about another tool that is great for testing the usability of the application directly from the physical device without needing to build and install the application on the device.

3
Command-line Interface

Command-line interface (CLI) enables you to to start new projects more easily, build them for different platforms, and run PhoneGap applications on the real device or in an emulator with a single command. We are going to discuss the following topics:

- Introduction to command-line interface
- Creating a new project
- Managing the project
- Using PhoneGap Build

Introduction to a command-line interface

With the introduction of the CLI to PhoneGap, things have become a lot easier as, previously, you needed to install the full IDE environment for a specific platform and then install an extension for PhoneGap to be able to create a PhoneGap hybrid application. If you wanted to support multiple platforms at the same time, it usually involved copying the mobile application resources and assets among them.

Command line has changed all that. Now, you can create a new project with a single command and then run the application in your browser in order to test the functionality before wrapping and building it for a specific platform. With another command, you can run the application in the platform emulator on your computer or run it natively on the physical device. Everything can be accomplished with just a few commands and all the development is done in your favorite text editor without the need to open another IDE to build and run for that specific platform.

PhoneGap CLI versus Cordova CLI

As the difference between PhoneGap and Cordova is minimal, there is confusion about PhoneGap's CLI and Cordova's CLI. Both are quite similar and you can get easily confused about which to use. The documentation for PhoneGap does not help as there are a lot of references to the Cordova command line, which adds even more misunderstandings to it.

The PhoneGap command line used the Cordova command line as its foundation but it was not always up-to-date with Cordova's latest commands; so all the commands that work in the Cordova command line might not work in the PhoneGap's command line. So, always check out which commands PhoneGap supports by visiting the PhoneGap API documentation web page `http://docs.phonegap.com` and make sure that you select the PhoneGap version that you are currently using. It is recommended that you update to the latest versions regularly.

Besides inconsistency with the command support, another big difference is the PhoneGap's included support for the PhoneGap Build service. The PhoneGap Build service allows you to compile your application directly on their servers rather than locally, which means that you can build an application for any major platform even if the operating system doesn't allow you to build it.

These two are the major differences between them; all the other differences are minor and do not affect your workflow. There is some remapping of the commands but this should not be anything too serious. In this chapter, all we will need is to open the command terminal where we will execute the commands.

Installing the PhoneGap CLI

There is no additional step to install the PhoneGap command-line interface if you have followed the instructions to prepare the development environment. It is already included in the PhoneGap library.

Creating a new project

The ability to create a new project with a single command can be a powerful and easy thing to do and so this is one of the most important additions in the command-line interface. It will create the full application structure and you will be ready to start building the app.

Creating a Hello project

Creating a basic project is easy and simple by running the following command:

```
phonegap create Hello
```

This will create a new `Hello` directory in the current directory for a project named Hello. You should get the following response:

```
MacBook-Air:Phonegap ivanturkovic$ phonegap create Hello
Creating a new cordova project with name "Hello World" and id "com.phonegap.helloworld" at location "/Users/ivanturkovic/Projects/Phonegap/Hello"

Using custom www assets from https://github.com/phonegap/phonegap-app-hello-world/archive/master.tar.gz
```

This will create the default directory file structure by convention. Some media assets will be included even though we have not yet defined which platform we will support. It should look as follows:

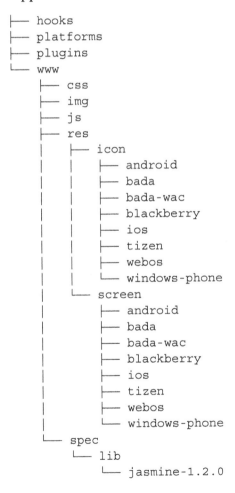

```
├── hooks
├── platforms
├── plugins
└── www
    ├── css
    ├── img
    ├── js
    ├── res
    │   ├── icon
    │   │   ├── android
    │   │   ├── bada
    │   │   ├── bada-wac
    │   │   ├── blackberry
    │   │   ├── ios
    │   │   ├── tizen
    │   │   ├── webos
    │   │   └── windows-phone
    │   └── screen
    │       ├── android
    │       ├── bada
    │       ├── bada-wac
    │       ├── blackberry
    │       ├── ios
    │       ├── tizen
    │       ├── webos
    │       └── windows-phone
    └── spec
        └── lib
            └── jasmine-1.2.0
```

Creating a new project

The command line can be more powerful in creating new applications by adding additional parameters while running the command.

Each part of the application can be customized such as the application name and package ID. These two parameters are important in the later stages of development, especially for the deployment, as these values are set up in the file called app manifest. This file can be found at ./www/config.xml and is used when creating native projects for specific platforms that are located inside ./platforms/<platform>/. The package ID is the identifier that will be used to sign the application while building for the deployment of the application binary to the app store:

```
phonegap create [options] <path> [id] [name] [config]
```

Basically, all the parameters are optional except the path where you create a new project. Let's go over the most important parameters, as follows:

- **options**: There are few available options to fine tune our new project:
    - `--name <name>`: It specifies the application name.
    - `--id <package>`: It specifies the package name ID. If this is missing, it defaults to com.phonegap.hello-world. It should follow a similar reverse domain name notation for the package ID.
    - `--template <name>`: By providing the name of the template, PhoneGap will create a new project from that template.
    - `--copy-from <path>`: It will create a new project by copying the whole file structure of an existing PhoneGap application that can be modified and edited without changing the original project. This is useful if you have a boilerplate project prepared for your favorite stack of tools that you are using in the project.
    - `--src <path>`: It does the same thing as the copy-from parameter.
    - `--link_to <path>`: The link_to parameter links the new project to another project that already has a working code. This is useful if you want to try out new configurations or change the settings in any of the platforms without the worry that you might break something and need to rebuild it from the beginning for a specific platform.
- **id**: It is just shorthand writing for the options ID setting.
- **name**: It is just shorthand writing for the options name setting.
- **config**: It provides you with the ability to pass a JSON string with additional settings that will be injected into ./.cordova/config.json file.

The following are examples of using the PhoneGap `create` command:

- To create an application with the `PhoneGap Essentials` name in the essentials directory and the `com.phonegap-essentials` package ID, use the following code:

```
phonegap create essentials --name "PhoneGap Essentials" --id "com.
phonegap-essentials"
```

- The preceding command can be used in shorthand as well:

```
phonegap create essentials "PhoneGap Essentials" "com.phonegap-
essentials"
```

- To make a copy of the existing application with a new package ID named `com.phonegap-advanced`, you can copy the existing application in it. For example, if we are in the same directory that we used in order to run the previous command, you will just need to run the following command:

```
phonegap create advanced —id "com.phonegap-advanced" —copy-from ./
essentials
```

All the settings that we passed through the command can be changed later by changing the content of the `config.xml` file, and so it is easy to update or rename later in case you need to do this.

Managing platforms

Creating a new project is pretty much empty and it does not do a lot until you specify which platforms you would like your application to support; thus, we need to add each platform separately. Currently, PhoneGap supports the following platforms; the platform keyword to add the platform is mentioned in the brackets:

- iOS (ios)
- BlackBerry (blackberry10)
- Android (android)
- Amazon Fire OS (amazon-fireos)
- webOS (webos)
- Windows Phone (windows for version 7 and wp8 for version 8)
- Symbian OS (symbian)
- Tizen - (tizen)
- Bada (bada)
- Firefox OS (firefoxos)
- Ubuntu Touch (ubuntu)
- Web browser (browser)

These platforms can be added at any time and there is no limitation on using multiple ones at the same time. You just need to check whether each plugin supports the added platform. We will go more detail about this in the next chapter.

All the commands to manage the platform have in common the start of the command:

```
phonegap platform <command> <options>
```

All commands should be run in the root folder of the PhoneGap project to be able to work, except the command to create a new PhoneGap project, which can be run anywhere.

Adding a platform

Adding a new platform is simple with the add command. The only parameter that it accepts is a single or multiple names of the platforms that we want to add. The add command can accept the platform name or file path, as follows:

```
phonegap platform add ios
```

To add two platforms at the same time, run the following command:

```
phonegap platform add ios android
```

Listing platforms

To list all the currently installed and available platforms for your application, you can run the following command:

```
phonegap platform list
```

Removing a platform

In some cases, we do not want to support some of the platforms and decide to remove it from the list of platforms with the remove command. In our example, we will remove android. Run the following command:

```
phonegap platform remove android
```

Keeping platforms up-to-date

As per the previous recommendation about keeping the PhoneGap command line updated to the latest version, it is recommended to have the platforms updated as well in order to reflect the latest build version for a specific platform.

First, we will run the following command:

```
phonegap platform check
```

If there is an empty response, it means that there are no pending updates for any platform. In case you get a list of platforms to update, you should run the following command to update it. We will use the android platform, which we want to update:

```
phonegap platform update android
```

After you update the platforms, they will have the latest changes and bug fixes that should make your applications more stable and future-proof.

Application description

There are many occasions when you need to get a quick glance at the full details about the project and the platforms or plugins that you are currently using. With a single command, we can print out a report that summarizes the current system and application setup from config.xml:

```
phonegap info
```

This command will create the same output in the info.txt file in the project root, which you can freely delete as there is not much use for it.

Creating a project from a template

When you create a new project, it is pretty much boilerplate without any additional functionality. This can be changed with the prototype that is provided when creating the new project. A full list of the templates that are available on your computer can be obtained by running the following command:

```
phonegap template list
```

The default installation should have only two basic templates:

- **blank**: A blank and empty PhoneGap app
- **hello-world**: The default hello world app for PhoneGap

The template name can be inserted when we are creating the new project:

```
phonegap create Hello -template hello-world
```

Managing the project

After creating the project, there are many things that we need to do to make sure that we have a working application as we need to prepare and later build the application in a usable state. We will cover these steps in this section.

Application preview

When the project is in development, building it in a native application and deploying it to the physical device can be time-consuming, especially if we do a lot of updates among the user tests. Preparing and building the whole application code that is required for wrapping a hybrid application in a native application takes time to execute.

PhoneGap has a really useful command that you will be using the most while developing the application. It basically creates a local Node.js web server with the live reload functionality that serves the application's content similar to a regular web page. The application works the same way as it does on the mobile device but in this case we are running it in the testing environment.

It was intended to be used with the PhoneGap Developer app but as it is a regular web server and web browser, you can open it on a specific port. I would recommend that you use the Google Chrome web browser as it has great development tools for debugging the pages.

Running a local web server with the content of the application is simple by running the following command:

```
phonegap serve
```

The app will run by default on port 3000. It will auto-reload the current page if it detects changes in any of the JavaScript, CSS, or HTML files. To run it inside the web browser, just open the http://localhost:3000 page.

There are a few options that can be used with the command; however, only one is worth mentioning: assigning a different port number. For example, if we want to run on 4000, we will run the following command:

```
phonegap serve -p 4000
```

The command will run until it is interrupted by the keyboard shortcut *Ctrl* + *Z*.

Though it is quite useful, it is worth knowing that it is not meant to be used for testing everything in a computer's web browser. The features that require a native API are not reachable, so this mode is useful for building and testing the user interface while mocking the features that are native in nature.

Preparing an application

Before building an application, all the required source code and assets need to be copied to a specific platform in order to have the latest source code. As there are more advanced commands for building applications, this command is useful if we want to manually build them in the IDE as opposed to using the command-line building process.

To be able to prepare the web assets from the www/ directory, we need to run the following command:

```
phonegap prepare
```

You are going to use this frequently, but there are times when you want to prepare a specific platform. You can optionally list them as shown in the following command, where we will prepare the assets only from the android platform:

```
phonegap prepare android
```

Once this process has been done, the project is ready to be compiled in a binary application by running the compile command or manually building it in the IDE. As mentioned before, this command is not usually used but it can be used in a build or run command.

Compiling an application

After finishing the process of preparing the web assets in specific directories for every platform, we will want to compile the actual code. The project is ready for us to compile a binary application that can be run on the devices. The easiest way to compile after the project is prepared is to run the following command:

```
phonegap compile
```

This will, by default, compile all the platforms that are available for the project unless we state a specific platform that we want to build. For example, if we want to compile a binary application only for android, we run the following command:

```
phonegap compile android
```

As both of the commands are related, we might want to run both of them one after another and so it is better to run both of them in a single line, as shown in the following command:

```
phonegap prepare android && phonegap compile android
```

Building an application

As the previous command is quite common, we have unified it in a single command that prepares the web assets and then compiles it in a binary application. The simplest method is to run the following command:

```
phonegap build
```

However, this is not a recommended way to build the application as it builds a binary application for every single platform that is added to the project. Usually you test the functionality on a single platform device, as building for every single platform takes a lot of time, especially if you have three or more platforms for the existing project. The following example builds a binary application for the android platform:

```
phonegap build android
```

I would recommend that you run it with a single platform of developing the application. When the features are done and the application moves to the intensive testing phase, you should build all the platforms at the same time in order to be prepared to install them on the various devices.

There are other commands that are available to automate the process while developing a PhoneGap application. The process of building a binary application directly without running it is usually reserved when you want to send it to other people so that they can test it on their devices.

Another time when you need to run the `build` command is when you make a release version of the binary application that is ready for deployment to the application store. You can prepare a release version by running the command with the `-release` option. This command prepares the unsigned release APK file as follows:

```
phonegap build android —release
```

Default settings will create an APK file in the debug mode, whereas adding the `release` option flag will create the APK file in the release mode.

Running an application

Building an application and manually installing it on the device can be time-consuming, so there is another command that does all the work for you. The `run` command is an all-in-one command that prepares all the web assets for the selected platforms. It compiles the assets in an installable application. After compilation, you can install it in the actual device or an emulator. To run the default application, run the following command:

```
phonegap run
```

As this process involves processor-intensive tasks, it is not recommended that you run it. You will need to attach a device for every platform that you are building at the same time. It is easier to try the application on a single platform; for example, on android, you can run the following command:

```
phonegap run android
```

As this is the most simple yet a powerful command when running the application, it has a few more options that you can use based on your needs:

- `-device`: This command is used if you need to build and install the application on the physical device, as follows:

  ```
  phonegap run android —device
  ```

  In the following chapters, we will cover in detail about how to setup your environment in order to connect your mobile device to the computer.

- `-emulator`: This command is used if you want to build and run the application in the emulator in your computer and since emulator is memory- and processor-intensive, it might affect your computer's performance and it is recommended that you do not use emulators with a high-screen resolution as the performance might be affected a lot. Run the following command:

  ```
  phonegap run android —emulator
  ```

- `-release`: This is used if you need to build a release version of the application and test it at the same time in the device or emulator. This is the last preview of the application before it is sent for submission to the app store. However, this may not always run in the emulator as the release version is usually built for a different processor's architecture that the computer runs. For example, run the following command:

  ```
  phonegap run android —release
  ```

- `-nobuild`: The `nobuild` option is useful if you have already built the application before and just want to run it in the device. Building the application is the most time-consuming part so if there were no changes in the code, then you can run the application faster. It is also great for testing on multiple devices sequentially. After you are done testing with one platform, you can run it on another one. An example for running nobuild on an Android is as follows:

  ```
  phonegap run android —nobuild
  ```

Emulating an application

Most of the time, it is easier to run the application in the emulator if we do not need to access the device-specific sensors that are not available in the emulator. There is a command that is shorthand for a PhoneGap run: -emulator. Instead, you can just call a single command to run the application in the emulator, such as the following command:

```
phonegap emulate
```

As this command involves processor-intensive tasks for building an application for every platform, it is not recommended that you run as it stands, as you need to have running emulators for each platform that you are building at the same time. It is easier to try the application in a single emulator, for example, in android:

```
phonegap emulate android
```

As this is the most simple yet a powerful command when running the application, it has a few more options, which you can use based on your needs:

- -release: This is used if you need to build a release version of the application and test it in the emulator. This is the last preview of the application before it is sent for submission to the app store. However, this may not always run in the emulator as the release version is usually built for a different processor's architecture that the computer runs. The following example will prepare the release version that will be run in the emulator:

  ```
  phonegap emulate android —release
  ```

- -nobuild: The nobuild option is useful if you have already built the application before and just want to run it in the device. Building the application is the most time-consuming part so if there were no changes in the code, you can run application faster. It is also great for testing on multiple devices sequentially and after done testing with one platform run on another one. An example for running nobuild on an Android is as follows:

  ```
  phonegap run android —nobuild
  ```

Using PhoneGap Build

PhoneGap Build is one of the major differences between PhoneGap and Cordova. This applies to the PhoneGap command-line interface, which has a built-in support for PhoneGap Build. The PhoneGap command-line is able to build binary applications remotely with the help of PhoneGap Build.

There are various reasons why this is more useful than building them locally. The main reason is that PhoneGap Build has the built-in support for building binary applications only for the following platforms:

- iOS
- Android
- Windows Phone

While there are just three platforms, it is worth mentioning that if you use local PhoneGap, Windows applications can be built only on the Windows computer, iOS applications can be built on Mac OS computers only, and Android can be built on any operating system. While using PhoneGap Build, you can build for all three platforms, no matter which OS you are using.

Another reason for building remotely is faster collaboration, team members and roles can be added to anyone, and applications can be sent to testers directly. These are all the features that can come in useful if you are working in a large team; however, if you are working alone or in a small group, these advantages are not immediately noticeable.

Authentication

Before you start to work with PhoneGap Build, you need to have an account. If you do not have an Adobe ID, go to `http://build.phonegap.com` and follow the **Sign up** link to create a new account there.

To start working with remote building, first we need to authenticate the command line with our Adobe account with the following command:

```
phonegap remote login
```

This command will request you for your username (your e-mail) and password, as follows:

```
MacBook-Air:Hello ivanturkovic$ phonegap remote login
[phonegap] PhoneGap/Build Login
[phonegap] Sign up at build.phonegap.com
 [warning] GitHub accounts are unsupported
  [prompt] enter username:          @gmail.com
  [prompt] enter password:
[phonegap] logged in as          @gmail.com
```

Now you will be logged in until you decide to log out. In case you need to log out, you just have to run the following command:

```
phonegap remote logout
```

Preparing the application

By default PhoneGap Build will try to generate applications for every platform that it supports. Specify the optional `<gap:platform>` element in the `config.xml` file if you want to make only certain platforms available. The following element shows the available values for the specific platform:

- The iOS tag element is `<gap:platform name="ios" />`
- The Android tag element is `<gap:platform name="android" />`
- The Windows tag element is `<gap:platform name="windows" />`

These optional tag elements are inserted in the root document of the `config.xml` file for the platforms that you want; PhoneGap Build will remotely build them for you.

Another difference with the locally built binary applications is that you need to specify in the `config.xml` file an optional `<gap:plugin>` element for every feature you want in the remotely built projects. For example, to add the `SplashScreen` feature, you need to add the following tag element to the root structure:

```
<gap:plugin name="SplashScreen" value="org.apache.cordova.core.
SplashScreen" />
```

Building the application

The next step is to build the binary application remotely. Building an installable application for a specific platform is available through PhoneGap remote build command. With the following command you can build the Android app for our example:

```
phonegap remote build android
```

This will upload the source code and build the application remotely. In case there is no application with the package ID in our PhoneGap Build list, it will create a new app there too. So, if you log in to `http://build.phonegap.com/` on the dashboard, you should see your newly-built application too.

The main advantage of building the binary application locally is to be able to install it in any device as long it is available as a URL or QR code. To build and run the application on the android platform, you will need to run the following command:

```
phonegap remote run android
```

It will update the code from the local web assets, build the binary application for the specified platform, and return a QR code in the terminal. You can use your phone to scan the QR code in order to receive the actual download link for the application, which you can then install in your device, as shown in the following screenshot:

```
Ivans-MacBook-Pro:hello ivanturkovic$ phonegap remote run android
[phonegap] compressing the app...
cp: dest file already exists: /Users/ivanturkovic/Projects/hello/build/www/config.xml

[phonegap] uploading the app...
[phonegap] building the app...
[phonegap] Android build complete
[phonegap] generating the QRCode...
```

Summary

In this chapter, you learned about PhoneGap's command-line interface and how it can be used throughout the full workflow of creating new PhoneGap applications. It can be used from the beginning until deployment, which has simplified the process of manually creating and building applications for each mobile platform separately.

We covered all the main commands that are needed to be able to prepare the PhoneGap application for deployment to the app store and how to use PhoneGap Build directly from the command line.

In the next chapter, we will go in detail about the plugins for PhoneGap.

4
Plugin Support

The access to any platform API is disabled by default, so all the features are nicely packed in separate plugins that you can add and manage based on your needs. There are two ways of managing them, using the Cordova command-line interface or being specific for each platform using Plugman (`https://github.com/apache/cordova-plugman`). This chapter will cover the following topics:

- Introducing plugins
- The command-line interface
- Plugman
- npm
- Plugins

Introducing plugins

PhoneGap was created with an idea to be able to create a hybrid application that is portable over different mobile platforms, while being able to use the features that are limited to the native devices. This could not be possible without the plugins that are responsible for invoking native method calls from the commands that are coming from the JavaScript in a PhoneGap application.

The core idea of building hybrid mobile applications with PhoneGap is to be able to create applications that are portable across different mobile platforms, which is achieved with the different plugins that are available. A wide range of plugins is available for PhoneGap depending on your needs; they provide you with the ability to do things that are reserved for the native applications.

Plugins are developed on a one-for-each mobile platform basis, which means not all plugins support the out-of-the-box platforms. However, most of the popular plugins support iOS and Android. All the Cordova plugins that are managed by the Apache Foundation support all three major mobile platforms: iOS, Android, and Windows.

Starting with version 3.0, API access to the native features is separated from the core PhoneGap by plugins, which means that PhoneGap doesn't provide any plugin installed by default and so it needs to be managed either by the command-line interface, Git repository, plugman, or npm, the new upcoming standard for plugins. When you create a new PhoneGap project, it does not have any plugins present. This is the new default behavior. Any plugins that you need, even the core plugins, must be explicitly added.

What is a plugin?

A plugin is an extension of the core PhoneGap that provides you with the ability to communicate with native components directly from JavaScript. With plugins, a PhoneGap application can behave like a native application without the need to write the native code.

Another advantage is that you can write code that invokes the native features and then make it work with any mobile platform that has support from the plugin. There are hundreds of plugins that cover many native features but in case there is one missing, you are free to develop your own plugin. However, keep in mind that creating a usable plugin requires you to have a deep knowledge of developing code for at least the iOS and Android platforms, as the code that communicates with the native API needs to be written in native code for the specific platform. Unless you need to create a plugin for internal use, you would need to know three different languages: Java for Android, Objective-C or Swift for iOS, and C# for Windows phone.

Every plugin has a unique plugin ID that is identified and used for installing the plugin.

Support for different mobile platforms

A plugin does not have to support every mobile platform. It is up to the creator of the plugin to decide which mobile platform to support. A vast majority of plugins have limited support and usually support only the iOS and Android mobile platforms at the moment while some others have even more limited support. The most popular plugins generally support all three major platforms.

Installing plugins

There are two ways to manage plugins for the application. Both of them can be used to achieve the same basic workflows in order to create a mobile app. You can use either workflow to accomplish the same task. They each offer the following advantages:

- **Cross-platform workflow**: The PhoneGap's **command-line interface** (CLI) tool is used to add plugins, which enables you to manage multiple mobile platforms at the same time
- **Platform-centered workflow**: The Plugman's CLI tool is on a lower level and is used to manage each mobile platform separately

Command-line Interface

Installing plugins through the PhoneGap's CLI is useful when you want to run the same configuration for different mobile platforms with almost no need for specific settings for any of them. CLI is a high-level utility that automatically copies sets among different mobile platforms, sets up all the settings, and builds the required application binaries.

The common interface enables you to apply plugins easily to multiple mobile platforms at the same time. This is the preferred way of managing plugins for a PhoneGap application now, and Plugman serves if you need more platform-specific settings.

Finding plugins

CLI has a simple command where you can find the plugin that you are looking for by the keyword. The plugins that are available in the search are residing in the Cordova Plugin Registry service and are identified by the plugin ID. (All the commands except creating a new project should be run in the working directory for a project).

```
phonegap plugin search <keyword>
```

For example, if you search for the `status` keyword, it will list the various plugins that have the `status` keyword:

```
MacBook-Air:hello ivanturkovic$ phonegap plugin search status
com.blueshift.cordova.battery - Battery
com.connectivity.monitor - Connectivity status monitoring. Detects if there is WIFI/3G/EDGE/CDMA available.
com.internrocket.plugins.statusbarcolor - Change the status bar color in Android Lollipop

com.onsip.sipjs - [![Build Status](https://travis-ci.org/onsip/SIP.js.png?branch=master)](https://travis-ci.org/onsip/SIP.js)
com.patrickheneise.cordova.statusbar - Cordova Status Bar Plugin
com.sudi.plugins.tintstatusbar -
    Tint the Android status bar

de.appplant.cordova.plugin.hidden-statusbar-overlay - Cordova 3.x.x plugin to hide the statusbar and overlay on iOS
org.apache.cordova.battery-status - Cordova Battery Plugin
org.apache.cordova.statusbar - Cordova StatusBar Plugin
org.chromium.idle - This plugin provides the ability to listen and check for the idle status of a device.
org.chromium.notifications - This plugin allows apps to show notifications in the status bar.
```

Adding plugins

Once you find the plugin that fits the needs of the application, it can be installed with a simple command. Every plugin is identified by the plugin ID:

```
phonegap plugin add <plugin id>
```

For example, if we want to install the `status bar` from the previous search that goes by the plugin ID `org.apache.cordova.statusbar`, we run the following command, as shown in the following screenshot:

```
MacBook-Air:hello ivanturkovic$ phonegap plugin add org.apache.cordova.statusbar
Fetching plugin "org.apache.cordova.statusbar" via plugin registry
```

Besides adding plugins by the plugin ID, plugins can be added from the remote Git repository as well, typically a GitHub repository:

```
phonegap plugin add <full git repository url>
```

You can simply add a plugin from the local directory as well. This is suitable if you are developing your own plugin or downloading a source for the plugin:

```
phonegap plugin add <full path to directory>
```

Listing plugins

It is simple to list all the currently installed plugins for the application by running the following command:

```
phonegap plugin ls
```

It will list the currently installed plugins; in the case of our example, it will return the previously installed plugin:

```
MacBook-Air:hello ivanturkovic$ phonegap plugin ls
org.apache.cordova.statusbar 0.1.10 "StatusBar"
```

Removing plugins

You can easily remove plugins from an application with the following command:

```
phonegap plugin rm <plugin ID>
```

We can remove the plugin that we installed previously with the following command:

```
MacBook-Air:hello ivanturkovic$ phonegap plugin rm org.apache.cordova.statusbar
Removing "org.apache.cordova.statusbar"
```

Plugman

The Plugman utility is used when you need to set up plugins for various mobile platforms that differ in their requirements. In this case, every mobile platform can be custom-made to respond to the requirements and be updated separately.

This comes in handy even if you have the same plugin and there are some bugs specific to a single platform that are causing the whole app to crash for that mobile platform. So, in this case, the older version can be used for the specific platform until it is resolved.

In general, this gives you the ability to make custom cross-platform applications. However, it is more difficult due to the lack of common tasks, such as building binaries or updating the plugin versions that are handled separately.

There is another side of the Plugman utility that is useful for developers who want to develop their own plugin. The Plugman utility has the commands that are able to create the basics needed for the plugin and for publishing it as well.

Installing Plugman

The prerequisites to install the Plugman utility are Node.js and git. If you have followed the instructions on how to install PhoneGap, then you only need to install the Plugman utility with the following command:

```
npm install -g plugman
```

After you execute the previous command, you can run the following command:

```
plugman
```

This should print out the help information about every command the utility supports. If you cannot view it, please revisit *Chapter 2, Mobile Platform Support,* and install it for your operating system.

Searching for plugins

Similar to the CLI for plugins, you can search for the existing plugins from the same plugin repository with the following command:

```
plugman search <keyword>
```

After searching for the keyword, it returns the same plugin results, as follows:

```
MacBook-Air:hello ivanturkovic$ plugman search status
com.blueshift.cordova.battery - Battery
com.connectivity.monitor - Connectivity status monitoring. Detects if there is WIFI/3G/EDGE/CDMA available.
com.internrocket.plugins.statusbarcolor - Change the status bar color in Android Lollipop
com.onsip.sipjs - [![Build Status](https://travis-ci.org/onsip/SIP.js.png?branch=master)](https://travis-ci.org/onsip/SIP.js)
com.patrickheneise.cordova.statusbar - Cordova Status Bar Plugin
com.sudi.plugins.tintstatusbar -
    Tint the Android status bar

de.appplant.cordova.plugin.hidden-statusbar-overlay - Cordova 3.x.x plugin to hide the statusbar and overlay on iOS
org.apache.cordova.battery-status - Cordova Battery Plugin
org.apache.cordova.statusbar - Cordova StatusBar Plugin
org.chromium.idle - This plugin provides the ability to listen and check for the idle status of a device.
org.chromium.notifications - This plugin allows apps to show notifications in the status bar.
```

Installing plugins

Once you find the plugin that fits the needs of the application, it can be installed with a simple command. Every plugin is identified by the plugin ID. The only difference is that you need to provide a platform you want to install it on:

```
plugman install —platform <ios|android|…> —project <full path to
directory> —plugin <plugin ID> [—variable NAME=VALUE]
```

Plugman command supports the following options:

- `platform`: This is one of the android, ios, blackberry10, wp7, or wp8 platforms.

- `project`: This is the path reference to a PhoneGap-generated project on the platform that you specify.

- `plugin`: This is one of the path references to a local copy of a plugin or a remote `https:` or `git:` URL that points to a Cordova plugin or a plugin ID from the Cordova Plugin Registry.

- `variable NAME=VALUE`: Some plugins require the install-time variables to be defined. These could be things like the API keys/tokens or other app-specific variables.

In this example, we will install the status bar plugin with the plugin ID using the following command:

```
plugman install —platform iOS —plugin org.apache.cordova.statusbar
```

Removing plugins

Removing plugins from the application is easy with the following command:

```
plugman uninstall —platform <ios|android|...> —plugin <plugin ID>
```

We will replace the plugin that we installed in the previous example with a status bar plugin with the plugin ID, `org.apache.cordova.statusbar`:

```
plugman uninstall —platform iOS —plugin org.apache.cordova.statusbar
```

npm

In April 2015, the Apache Cordova team decided to move their official plugin source to the `http://www.npmjs.com` repository. It is good to know that the existing way of hosting plugins will be deprecated in the near future. In this book, I am going to try to include both plugin IDs for the existing and future support as all the plugins are not yet available through `npm`, especially the third-party libraries. The `npm` plugins are available for installation with the release of PhoneGap version 5.0 and it will become the default source of the plugins.

The PhoneGap's core plugins will change their IDs from `org.apache.cordova.*` to `cordova-plugin-*`.

There will be no change in the handling of the new plugin installation; you will use the same command, only the plugin ID will determine where the plugin will be installed from. All the functionalities and behaviors will remain the same; it is good to know that npm will become the default plugin library in the future. Once the transition is done, you will need to use only npm plugins.

Plugins

Currently, you can get over a thousand different plugins for different functionalities. These plugins usually support only selected mobile platforms because for the plugins to work on every platform, they have to contain a native code for that specific mobile platform in order to get executed. The majority of the plugins support the iOS and Android mobile platforms; support for other platforms is not so widespread.

There is a service called Apache Cordova Plugins Registry (`http://plugins.cordova.io`) where you can find all the plugins listed in a single location, as shown in the following screenshot. These plugins can be searched and filtered based on your needs:

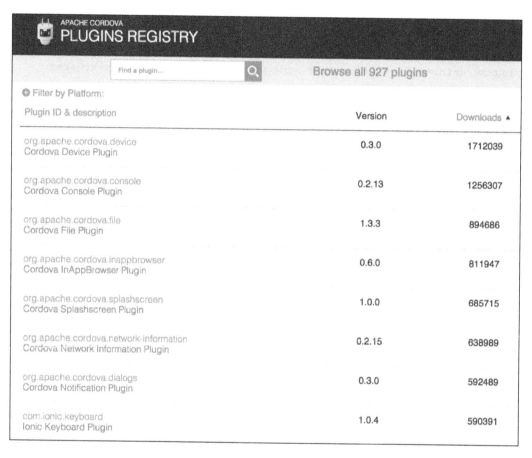

It is very easy to find the popular plugins for your needs by entering the functionality in a search query and then sorting it by the number of downloads.

We will make a quick overview of the useful plugins that work on most of the mobile platforms. The list of plugins is sorted alphabetically for easier access.

Battery Status

The battery status provides you with a monitoring capability of a device's battery that enables you to check the battery status at any time. It gives you notifications for any changes in the battery capacity, which is useful when the battery level is critical and so you can save all the important data before the battery goes off.

- **Plugin ID**: `org.apache.cordova.battery-status`
- **Npm plugin ID**: `cordova-plugin-battery-status`

Camera

The camera plugin has the ability to access a native controller for taking photographs with the device's camera. It usually presents the default photograph-taking interface that is provided for the specific platform. Besides taking photographs, it provides you with the ability to select photographs from the native image library component.

- **Plugin ID**: `org.apache.cordova.camera`
- **Npm plugin ID**: `cordova-plugin-camera`

Contacts

The contacts plugin provides you with access to the native contacts component. It provides you with the ability to retrieve contact information from the native contacts database, insert new contacts, or update the existing contacts. Some of the features are limited to selected mobile platforms.

- **Plugin ID**: `org.apache.cordova.contacts`
- **Npm plugin ID**: `cordova-plugin-contacts`

Device

The device plugin enables you to access specific device information. It gives you information about the current PhoneGap version, device's model, device's platform, device's UUID (which represents the unique device ID), and the device's version. This kind of information is useful for the various parts of the code where you need to check for the existence of supported features based on the mobile platform.

- **Plugin ID**: `org.apache.cordova.device`
- **Npm plugin ID**: `cordova-plugin-device`

The Device Motion plugin

The Device Motion plugin has the ability to use the internal sensor to measure the acceleration of the device. It emits events for acceleration changes or you can read the current values. It supports the watching of accelerations in the x, y, and z axes at specific intervals.

- **Plugin ID**: `org.apache.cordova.device-motion`
- **Npm plugin ID**: `cordova-plugin-device-motion`

Device position orientation

The device orientation plugin provides you with access to the internal device's compass. The compass is a sensor that detects the direction or heading that the device is pointed toward, typically from the top of the device. It measures the heading in degrees from 0 to 359.99, where 0 is north.

- **Plugin ID**: `org.apache.cordova.device-orientation`
- **Npm plugin ID**: `cordova-plugin-device-orientation`

Dialogs

The Dialogs plugin provides you with the ability to present native dialog components to the user. When you need to give the user an alert dialog box with an additional message or description, this plugin presents the user with a dialog box to confirm the action before continuing it. Most of the platforms use native components but some use the browser's dialogs.

- **Plugin ID**: `org.apache.cordova.dialogs`
- **Npm plugin ID**: `cordova-plugin-dialogs`

FileSystem

The FileSystem plugin implements the ability to access files from the native device. You can usually read or write files that are residing on the device. Different mobile platforms provide different file access, for example, iOS gives access to only those files that are residing in a sandboxed environment specifically for each application; it cannot access outside files.

- **Plugin ID**: `org.apache.cordova.file`
- **Npm plugin ID**: `cordova-plugin-file`

File Transfer

The File Transfer plugin integrates the upload and download of files directly from the Internet. For file uploads and downloads, it uses the HTTP POST request. While performing the upload or download, you can monitor the progress of the process, which you can abort altogether.

- **Plugin ID**: `org.apache.cordova.file-transfer`
- **Npm plugin ID**: `cordova-plugin-file-transfer`

Geolocation

The Geolocation plugin has the ability to locate the current user's location with the help of an integrated GPS sensor. It provides a location with its latitude and longitude. Besides getting the current location, you can also set events in order to follow the user's location updates.

- **Plugin ID**: `org.apache.cordova.geolocation`
- **Npm plugin ID**: `cordova-plugin-geolocation`

Globalization

The Globalization plugin obtains information and performs operations specific to the user's locale, language, currency, and time zone. There is a difference between locale and language: locale provides information about how to present and parse the local dates and other information while language is used to present the content in that language.

- **Plugin ID**: `org.apache.cordova.globalization`
- **Npm plugin ID**: `cordova-plugin-globalization`

InAppBrowser

The InAppBrowser plugin provides you with another browser in which you can open a web page directly from the application. This browser window behaves like a regular web browser, which means that it cannot access any PhoneGap-specific API. So, this is useful only when you want to load third-party content. It can open any web URL address that you provide.

- **Plugin ID**: `org.apache.cordova.inappbrowser`
- **Npm plugin ID**: `cordova-plugin-inappbrowser`

Media

The Media plugin provides you with the ability to record and play back audio files on a device. With this plugin, you can play internal or external audio files provided with the URL address as well. It provides almost full audio playback, as the native applications do; so you can play music in the background while using another application.

- **Plugin ID**: `org.apache.cordova.media`
- **Npm plugin ID**: `cordova-plugin-media`

Media Capture

The Media Capture plugin provides access to the various media input elements that the device possesses such as audio, image, and video capabilities. Every capability has a custom native application view in which you can record different media. The UI depends on the mobile platform.

- **Plugin ID**: `org.apache.cordova.media-capture`
- **Npm plugin ID**: `cordova-plugin-media-capture`

Network Information

The Network Information plugin provides you with the information that almost every application will need if it depends on the Internet connection. This plugin gives you the ability to check what kind of connection is currently available or if there is no connection at the moment. It also has events that can be triggered when the device goes into offline or online mode.

- **Plugin ID**: `org.apache.cordova.network-information`
- **Npm plugin ID**: `cordova-plugin-network-information`

Splashscreen

The Splashscreen plugin has a single feature and that is to show the splash screen image on loading and hide it when the app is already loaded. The splash screen is visible during the process of loading the data from the Internet connection and once it is downloaded, it can be hidden.

- **Plugin ID**: `org.apache.cordova.splashscreen`
- **Npm plugin ID**: `cordova-plugin-splashscreen`

Vibration

The Vibration plugin provides you with the capability of activating the internal device's vibrating feedback, which gives a silent reminder when it is needed. It can activate a simple vibration reminder or give a pattern of vibrations. You need to check out the platform compatibility.

Plugin ID: `org.apache.cordova.vibration`

Npm plugin ID: `cordova-plugin-vibration`

StatusBar

The StatusBar plugin provides the ability to control the visual and functional part of the native status bar. You can control what color the status bar will correspond to or you can have an overlay of the application in the status bar based on the mobile platform support.

- **Plugin ID**: `org.apache.cordova.statusbar`
- **Npm plugin ID**: `cordova-plugin-statusbar`

Summary

In this chapter, you learned that plugins are essential for the PhoneGap application to work beyond being a simple wrapper for web applications. Plugins give you the ability to communicate with the native components directly from the PhoneGap application.

Later, you learned that there are many ways of managing plugins, either directly with the command-line interface or with Plugman. At the time of writing, a transition for the default location was going on, so all plugins in the future are going to be hosted on the npmjs site.

In the next chapter, we will build our first PhoneGap application and learn the basics of how to run it.

First PhoneGap Application

5

This will be the first chapter dedicated to creating an application instead of providing tasks related to preparing or managing the application development process. In this chapter, we will discover how the application is structured and how to properly use it:

- Starting a new application
- Project folder structure
- Core PhoneGap events
- Essential plugins

Starting a new application

Until now we have been learning how to set up the environment, how we can use the **command-line interface** (**CLI**), and how to use the most basic plugins. Now, if we followed the installation process, we should be able to create our first application and see how it works. For the following chapters, we will be using the Android simulator or a native Android device for features that require native capability. All the code works on any platform or, in the case of plugins, on all platforms that support plugins. So let's get started and create our first PhoneGap application.

Creating a new application

We already know all the commands so, if a command used in the following chapters is not clear, please take a look at the previous chapters as all used commands are mentioned there.

1. Let's create our first application called HelloWorld with:

```
phonegap create HelloWorld
```

2. It should print the following response:

```
Ivans-MacBook-Pro:hello ivanturkovic$ phonegap create HelloWorld
Creating a new cordova project.
```

3. The next step is to go into the project with:

```
cd HelloWorld
```

4. If you list the content of the directory:

```
ls -l
```

It should print the following directory structure for your new PhoneGap project like this:

```
total 16
-rw-rw-r--   1 ivanturkovic  staff   4.8K Jun  1 19:58
config.xml
drwxr-xr-x   3 ivanturkovic  staff   102B Jun  1 19:58 hooks
drwxr-xr-x   2 ivanturkovic  staff    68B Jun  1 19:58 platforms
drwxr-xr-x   2 ivanturkovic  staff    68B Jun  1 19:58 plugins
drwxr-xr-x  10 ivanturkovic  staff   340B Jun  1 19:58 www
```

We see four different directories and a `config.xml` file for setting up a specific configuration for the application in general or for a specific platform. Let's run it to see how your first application looks; later, we will explore what each of the directories means and how to use them.

```
phonegap run android
```

Don't worry if you haven't added Android platform support before running it on Android; it does all this automatically. Here is a printout of all the actions it takes:

```
[phonegap] executing 'cordova platform add android'...
[phonegap] completed 'cordova platform add android'
[phonegap] executing 'cordova run android'...
```

Downloading the example code

You can download the example code files for all Packt books you have purchased from your account at http://www.packtpub.com. If you purchased this book elsewhere, you can visit http://www.packtpub.com/support and register to have the files e-mailed directly to you.

5. If you previously carried out the setup procedure, after a short moment you should see the following screen on the Android emulator:

We have seen this before so let's explore where this is coming from. Open the `root` folder of the project in your favorite text editor and open the `www/index.html` file. You should see the following HTML code:

```html
<!DOCTYPE html>
<html>
  <head>
    <meta charset="utf-8" />
    <meta name="format-detection" content="telephone=no" />
    <meta name="msapplication-tap-highlight" content="no" />
    <meta name="viewport" content="user-scalable=no,
      initial-scale=1, maximum-scale=1, minimum-scale=1,
        width=device-width, height=device-height,
          target-densitydpi=device-dpi" />
```

```
      <link rel="stylesheet" type="text/css" href="css/index.css" />
      <title>Hello World</title>
    </head>
    <body>
      <div class="app">
        <h1>PhoneGap</h1>
        <div id="deviceready" class="blink">
          <p class="event listening">Connecting to Device</p>
          <p class="event received">Device is Ready</p>
        </div>
      </div>
      <script type="text/javascript" src="cordova.js"></script>
      <script type="text/javascript" src="js/index.js"></script>
      <script type="text/javascript">
        app.initialize();
      </script>
    </body>
  </html>
```

This is actually the screen that opens when you run the simulator; changing anything will change the appearance of the application. Besides the HTML file, there is a JavaScript file that actually controls the changes: www/js/index.js.

```
var app = {
  // Application Constructor
  initialize: function() {
    this.bindEvents();
  },
  // Bind Event Listeners
  //
  // Bind any events that are required on startup. Common events are:
  // 'load', 'deviceready', 'offline', and 'online'.
  bindEvents: function() {
    document.addEventListener("deviceready", this.onDeviceReady,
      false);
  },
  // deviceready Event Handler
  //
  // The scope of 'this' is the event. In order to call the
    'receivedEvent'
  // function, we must explicitly call 'app.receivedEvent(...);'
  onDeviceReady: function() {
    app.receivedEvent("deviceready");
  },
  // Update DOM on a Received Event
  receivedEvent: function(id) {
    var parentElement = document.getElementById(id);
    var listeningElement =
      parentElement.querySelector(".listening");
```

```
      var receivedElement =
        parentElement.querySelector(".received");

      listeningElement.setAttribute("style", "display:none; ");
      receivedElement.setAttribute("style", "display:block; ");

      console.log("Received Event: " + id);
    }
  };
```

To explain the automatically generated example inside the index.html file, you run app.initialize() to start the process of listening for PhoneGap to load all the required plugins and libraries before you can start using PhoneGap features besides the HTML-related functionality.

PhoneGap fires the deviceready event when it loads all the requirements for the PhoneGap platform. This is where you can start using the provided plugin API to access the native functionality.

Setting up the initial code

Since this is an introduction to building PhoneGap applications, we will simplify the code and provide the minimum required to run the examples in this book. Here is the updated index.html page file, representing the minimal content needed to run the samples in the following chapters:

```
<!DOCTYPE html>
<html>
  <head>
    <meta charset="utf-8" />
    <meta name="format-detection" content="telephone=no" />
    <meta name="msapplication-tap-highlight" content="no" />
    <meta name="viewport" content="user-scalable=no,
      initial-scale=1, maximum-scale=1, minimum-scale=1,
        width=device-width, height=device-height,
          target-densitydpi=device-dpi" />
    <link rel="stylesheet" type="text/css" href="css/index.css" />
    <title>Hello World</title>
  </head>
  <body>
    <div id="phonegap">
    </div>
    <script type="text/javascript" src="cordova.js"></script>
    <script type="text/javascript" src="js/index.js"></script>
  </body>
</html>
```

Every application needs to load the `cordova.js` file first, if you want to use PhoneGap's plugin API; it also provides events when it is ready to use them. Next we simplify the `index.js` file and enter the following code that will set the div tag with the text `Device is ready` after PhoneGap is fully loaded and functional:

```
document.addEventListener("deviceready", function(event) {
    var element = document.getElementById("phonegap");
    element.innerHTML = "Device is ready";
}, false);
```

Since the generated content comes with CSS styles, we have to update the `css/index.css` file with the following rule:

```
#phonegap {
    text-align: center;
}
```

Now, if we run PhoneGap again on Android, we should see the following screen; this is pretty barebones, but supplies the information we need. Integrating different UI frameworks that exist and can be used within jQuery mobile, jQT, or Ionic (to name a few) is beyond the scope of this book.

In the following sections, we will use this as a starting point to explain different samples used by different plugins. But first let's go over the structure of the application folder.

Project folder structure

PhoneGap emphasizes convention over configuration when it comes to its project folder structure. There are four main folders and a configuration file called `config.xml`. The configuration file is where you can change different preferences of the application, such as the starting home screen, that will load first. Throughout the book we will use the default option for home screen page that is pointing to `index.html`.

There are four folders in the root structure:

- `hooks`: Contains all the scripts that are used to customize different PhoneGap commands. Any scripts added to these internal folders will be executed before and after the specific command that corresponds to the folder name. It is useful to create your own building process in case some manual work is required with some of the plugins. These features are meant for advanced users but it is worth explaining them since the folder is created by default.

- `platforms`: Inside this folder, new folders are created for each new platform that is added to the project; inside, the whole structure to build a native application for a specific device will be laid out. A specific folder can be opened in IDE for specific platforms; for example, iOS can be opened with Xcode as a regular Xcode project.

- `plugins`: Any added plugin will be extracted or copied into this folder.

- `www`: This is the main folder for all the assets that the application is using; during the build process, its content is copied into a specific platforms folder every time you do a new build. It usually contains HTML, JavaScript, CSS, and image assets required to build a real application. It also contains a `res` folder where you put all the resources that are platform-specific, such as the splash screen or application icons. A generated project structure already contains placeholder files for every supported platform. The final one is the spec folder, which contains tests.

Here you can see a full tree generated by the PhoneGap CLI, which is ready to start building your own hybrid application:

```
├── config.xml
├── hooks
│   └── README.md
├── platforms
```

```
├── plugins
└── www
    ├── css
    │   └── index.css
    ├── icon.png
    ├── img
    │   └── logo.png
    ├── index.html
    ├── js
    │   └── index.js
    ├── res
    │   ├── icon
    │   │   ├── android
    │   │   │   ├── icon-36-ldpi.png
    │   │   │   ├── icon-48-mdpi.png
    │   │   │   ├── icon-72-hdpi.png
    │   │   │   └── icon-96-xhdpi.png
    │   │   ├── bada
    │   │   │   └── icon-128.png
    │   │   ├── bada-wac
    │   │   │   ├── icon-48-type5.png
    │   │   │   ├── icon-50-type3.png
    │   │   │   └── icon-80-type4.png
    │   │   ├── blackberry
    │   │   │   └── icon-80.png
    │   │   ├── ios
    │   │   │   ├── icon-57-2x.png
    │   │   │   ├── icon-57.png
    │   │   │   ├── icon-72-2x.png
    │   │   │   └── icon-72.png
    │   │   ├── tizen
    │   │   │   └── icon-128.png
    │   │   ├── webos
    │   │   │   └── icon-64.png
    │   │   └── windows-phone
    │   │       ├── icon-173-tile.png
    │   │       ├── icon-48.png
    │   │       └── icon-62-tile.png
    │   └── screen
    │       ├── android
    │       │   ├── screen-hdpi-landscape.png
```

```
|        |       ├── screen-hdpi-portrait.png
|        |       ├── screen-ldpi-landscape.png
|        |       ├── screen-ldpi-portrait.png
|        |       ├── screen-mdpi-landscape.png
|        |       ├── screen-mdpi-portrait.png
|        |       ├── screen-xhdpi-landscape.png
|        |       └── screen-xhdpi-portrait.png
|        ├── bada
|        |   └── screen-portrait.png
|        ├── bada-wac
|        |   ├── screen-type3.png
|        |   ├── screen-type4.png
|        |   └── screen-type5.png
|        ├── blackberry
|        |   └── screen-225.png
|        ├── ios
|        |   ├── screen-ipad-landscape-2x.png
|        |   ├── screen-ipad-landscape.png
|        |   ├── screen-ipad-portrait-2x.png
|        |   ├── screen-ipad-portrait.png
|        |   ├── screen-iphone-landscape-2x.png
|        |   ├── screen-iphone-landscape.png
|        |   ├── screen-iphone-portrait-2x.png
|        |   ├── screen-iphone-portrait-568h-2x.png
|        |   └── screen-iphone-portrait.png
|        ├── tizen
|        |   └── README.md
|        ├── webos
|        |   └── screen-64.png
|        └── windows-phone
|            └── screen-portrait.jpg
├── spec
|   ├── helper.js
|   ├── index.js
|   └── lib
|       └── jasmine-1.2.0
|           ├── MIT.LICENSE
|           ├── jasmine-html.js
|           ├── jasmine.css
|           └── jasmine.js
└── spec.html
```

Core PhoneGap events

The latest version of PhoneGap doesn't come with any plugins installed by default so we can completely customize it for our needs; however, it does still come with a few events that are useful for making an initial hybrid mobile application. These basics are needed for properly managing the workflow of the application. We will examine the events that all major platforms support.

The deviceready event

This event is a must-have if you want to be able to use PhoneGap's functionality or any other plugin. The `deviceready` event is invoked when PhoneGap and all related resources are loaded and ready to be used.

Let's have a look at the example code:

```
document.addEventListener("deviceready", onDeviceReady, false);
function onDeviceReady() {
    // Now safe to use PhoneGap's APIs
}
```

The pause event

The `pause` event is triggered when the native platform puts the application into the background, for various reasons such as closing the application to go into the home screen or switching between applications. This is a great place to save any crucial information before the application is put into the inactive state and you cannot predict what will happen next.

Let's have a look at the example code:

```
document.addEventListener("pause", onPause, false);
function onPause() {
    // Handle the pause event
}
```

The resume event

The `resume` event is triggered when the native platform wakes up the application into the foreground. It signals that the user is using the application again and it is a great place to restore a previously stored state to continue where it left off last time.

Let's have a look at the example code:

```
document.addEventListener("resume", onResume, false);

function onResume() {
    // Handle the resume event
}
```

Essential plugins

Since, in the latest PhoneGap version, no plugins are added by default, it was decided to keep the app builds as small and lightweight as possible. We are free to enhance the app based on our needs, but this could be challenging for beginners as there are so many plugins it is hard to decide which ones to start with. I have selected a few that, in my opinion, are essential and should be included in the core. So let's go over them and see what capabilities they enable.

The Device plugin

The Device plugin defines a global device object that describes the device's hardware and software information. The Device plugin is available only after the `deviceready` event has been used.

```
phonegap plugin add cordova-plugin-device
```

After installing the plugin, let us create an example of how it could be used. Generally, it is used for testing for the specific platform or model:

```
document.addEventListener('deviceready', function(event) {
    var content = "";
    content += "Version: " + device.cordova + "<br/>";
    content += "Platform: " + device.platform + "<br/>";
    content += "Device Model: " + device.model + "<br/>";
    content += "Platform Version: " + device.version + "<br/>";
    content += "UUID: " + device.uuid + "<br/>";
    var element = document.getElementById("phonegap");
    element.innerHTML = content;
}, false);
```

Substitute this code inside `index.js` and run the application. It should print all the important information about your device and should look like this:

The Network Information plugin

The Network Information plugin gives you information about the current network state of the device and also the supporting events that are triggered when the network state changes from offline to online, and vice versa. It is useful to detect when you can access data from a remote server or use the network to sync data remotely.

This plugin has two events that come in really handy in detecting changes in network access: an offline event that triggers when the device is without a connection and an online event that triggers when the device is back online but you want to check what kind of connection it has. 2G connection speed is not the same as a Wi-Fi connection.

```
phonegap plugins add cordova-plugin-network-information
```

For a network example, we will display the network type that is currently available on the device and prepare for the event changes that update the current connection type:

```
document.addEventListener("deviceready", function(event) {
    checkConnection();
```

```
}, false);

document.addEventListener("offline", checkConnection, false);
document.addEventListener("online", checkConnection, false);

function checkConnection() {
  var networkState = navigator.connection.type;

  var states = {};
  states[Connection.UNKNOWN]   = "Unknown connection";
  states[Connection.ETHERNET]  = "Ethernet connection";
  states[Connection.WIFI] = "WiFi connection";
  states[Connection.CELL_2G]   = "Cell 2G connection";
  states[Connection.CELL_3G]   = "Cell 3G connection";
  states[Connection.CELL_4G]   = "Cell 4G connection";
  states[Connection.CELL]      = "Cell generic connection";
  states[Connection.NONE]      = "No network connection";

  var element = document.getElementById("phonegap");
  element.innerHTML = "Connection type: " + states[networkState];
}
```

Depending on your current connection, this should display the current connection type your device is connected to:

The StatusBar plugin

The StatusBar plugin provides a global object that can manage the visual part of a device's status bar and change its properties based on the needs of the application. It supports configuration in the `config.xml` file or can be controlled directly from within the code. There are many specific methods you can apply based on your needs but the most important is the ability to show or hide the status bar:

```
phonegap plugins add cordova-plugin-statusbar
```

The global object is called StatusBar and it has the following property:

- `isVisible`: Returns true or false depending on the current state of the status bar. StatusBar has many methods but we will only explore a few that are the most important and most useful:

- `styleDefault()`: Use it to set the default status bar design: dark text.

- `backgroundColorByName(colorName)`: Set the status bar color based on the name of the color. Supported colors are: black, darkGray, lightGray, white, gray, red, green, blue, cyan, yellow, magenta, orange, purple, and brown.

- `backgroundColorByHexString(hexString)`: Set the status bar color based on the hex value of the color. CSS shorthand is also supported.

- `hide()`: Hide the status bar completely.

- `show()`: Show the status bar and use the previous type. If this has not been set, it will use the default one.

The Dialogs plugin

Support for various dialogs is already integrated directly into the device's web browser inside PhoneGap, but there are other ways to present a modal dialog that corresponds to the native UI of the specific device and gives a more native feel to the application.

```
phonegap plugin add cordova-plugin-dialogs
```

The Dialogs plugin attaches a `navigator.notification` object to the global navigator object; it is available only after the `deviceready` event. The Dialogs plugin supports four different ways of presenting a dialog:

- `navigator.notification.alert(message, alertCallback, [title], [buttonName])`: Shows a custom alert box with predefined content with a message, title, button name, and a callback after the button has been pressed.

```
document.addEventListener("deviceready", function(event) {
    navigator.notification.alert(
```

```
        "This is an alert",
        alertDismissed,
        "Confirm",
        "OK"
    );
}, false);

function alertDismissed() {
    var element = document.getElementById("phonegap");
    element.innerHTML = "Alert has been dismissed";
}
```

The following sample will display Alert has been dismissed after you press the **OK** button. The following screenshots reflect this process:

Pressing the confirmation button should show the result of the action:

- `navigator.notification.confirm(message, confirmCallback, [title], [buttonLabels])`: Displays a customizable dialog box containing a message; a confirmation callback function that receives the index of the button pressed (if none is pressed, it is 0); the title of the dialog; and a string array for the names of the buttons. This is great for asking users to confirm an important action, such as deleting content. The following example is a modified alert example that returns different responses based on which button is pressed:

```
document.addEventListener("deviceready", function(event) {
    navigator.notification.confirm(
        "Do you want to delete this file",
        confirmDismissed,
        "Confirm deletion",
        ["Yes", "No"]
    );
}, false);

function confirmDismissed(index) {
    var element = document.getElementById("phonegap");
```

```
    if (index === 1) {
        element.innerHTML = "File was deleted";
    } else{
        element.innerHTML = "File deletion was cancelled";
    }
}
```

The following sample will display a different message irrespective of whether you provided confirmation. The following screenshots confirm this:

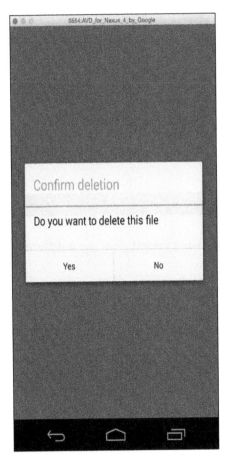

After providing confirmation, you should see the confirmation screen with your custom message:

If the cancel button was pressed, you see a different screen that is responding to the cancel action:

- `navigator.notification.prompt(message, promptCallback, [title], [buttonLabels], [defaultText])`: Behaves in a similar way to the confirm dialog with the exception that you can enter some string information. In our example, we will later display the information on the screen:

```
document.addEventListener("deviceready", function(event) {
    navigator.notification.prompt(
        "How do you want to name this text file",
        confirmDismissed,
        "File rename"
    );
}, false);

function confirmDismissed(results) {
    var element = document.getElementById("phonegap");
    element.innerHTML = "File was renamed to " + results.input1;
}
```

The following example will display the changed name based on the input you provided. In my case, I have entered `HelloWorld`:

And the response to the entered text will be the following screen showing your text input:

- `navigator.notification.beep(times)`: The device plays a beep sound; you can set how many times you want to repeat this beep.

Summary

In this chapter, we created our first PhoneGap application, explored how you can run your application, and learned about the basic structure of the application's project directory.

You learned how to build your first custom application, familiarized yourself with some basic plugins that you need to run your application, and acquired some basic information about your smartphone device.

6
Accessing Native APIs

In this chapter, we will be covering different native APIs that are available on most of the platforms that are supported (we will cover the following sensors: Accelerometer, Compass, and Geolocation):

- Native APIs
- Battery status
- Device Motion
- Device orientation
- Geolocation
- Globalization
- Vibration

Native APIs

Before PhoneGap, there were framework solutions that optimized web page content to fit on small screens, which were the norm back then. There were still restrictions compared to native applications, especially when it came to accessing native features, among them hardware sensors. This was before the proliferation of HTML5-standard features so there was really no way of accessing them without making a native application.

A wide array of hardware sensors supported through native APIs improves the functionality of hybrid mobile applications. Using them can replace the need to create a native application; this means it can cost less to develop a hybrid application than to build a separate version for all platforms that do not share any code, since every platform uses a different programming language. Plugins that we will explore in detail in the following chapters, are the main reason why the development of PhoneGap applications has risen in popularity. There are so many other plugins that extend support for specialized hardware features that are not yet part of the core PhoneGap plugins. In general, we divide them into four categories based on their functionality:

- Device status plugins
- Location-based plugins
- Media functionality plugins
- Notification plugins

For the following plugins, you need to have a real device to test on since most of the sensors don't work in the simulator. Some of the sensors can be tested inside web browsers that simulate them, but not all are supported. The process of running inside a device is the same as running on a simulator: just plug the device into a USB port and run the following command:

```
phonegap run android
```

I am using Android devices for these examples since they work on all platforms, but you can do the same with other platforms too. You need to pay special attention to the fact that some devices have development mode disabled by default; thus, please search online for how to enable development mode for your device since the procedure differs by model.

Device status plugins

Device status plugins give back information or trigger an event that is related to the inner working of the device. Here we are going to explain more about it by recourse to the Battery Status plugin, which returns the current charge of the battery.

Motion sensing plugins

There are many motion sensing plugins that give different data for different sensors inside the device under different circumstances. In this chapter, we are going to cover plugins for compass orientation, acceleration of the device in various directions, and GPS location data for orientation in the real world. These are all the location data that we would need for anything that is related to updating or searching.

Media functionality plugins

Media functionality plugins are a large group of plugins that range from media capture plugins for photos or videos, to retrieving existing media content. We are going to learn more about them in the next chapter since these plugins are an important part for creating an application.

Notification plugins

Notification plugins are another important group of plugins that return feedback to the user through different sources. In this chapter, we are going to take a look at the Vibration plugin, which emits a vibration to notify the user.

The Battery Status plugin

One of the important needs of an application is to know the current battery state so it can handle data correctly, and to ensure the battery does not run out before being able to save crucial data information, or take a crucial action.

There are three events that are especially useful for developing applications; they are related to the battery charge and determining when the battery state is critical, so you know when to save or back up data.

To install the following plugin, you need to run the following command:

```
phonegap plugin add cordova-plugin-battery-status
```

With this plugin, you need to run examples on the physical device since the simulator does not provide data for it. There are alternatives available, such as the Chrome browser with the Ripple plugin, but we will explore this in detail in the final chapter.

The Battery Status event

This event is emitted every time the battery charge changes by at least one percent or when the device is plugged or unplugged from charger. Event with two properties is passed into the callback function:

- `level`, which is the percentage of battery charge between 0 and 100
- `isPlugged`, a Boolean value that shows if the device is plugged in or not

In the following example, I will show you how to make a notification that responds to this event:

```
function onBatteryStatus(info) {
    alert("Battery Level: " + info.level + "\nDevice is plugged in: "
+ info.isPlugged);
}

document.addEventListener("'deviceready"', function(event) {
  window.addEventListener("batterystatus", onBatteryStatus, false);
});
```

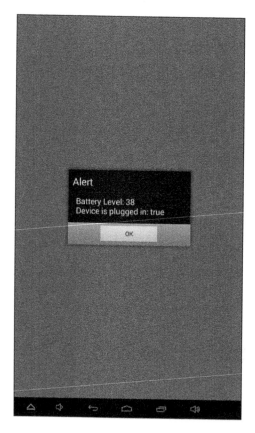

The Low Battery event

The Low Battery event behaves similarly to the Battery Status event with the exception that the event is emitted only when the device reaches a low battery threshold that is different, depending on the device plugin implementation.

The event handler function receives the same parameters as the previous event so we could reuse the same function as for the Battery Status event, if we are looking at battery changes, and respond to low values, so we can prepare for a further loss of charge in the future. The Low Battery event predicts that there is still enough battery for you to safely store the data but the Critical Battery event might turn off the device before you can do this in the event there is a lot of non-reproducible data.

In the following example, I will show you how to make a response to this event:

```
document.addEventListener("deviceready", function(event) {
    window.addEventListener("batterylow", onBatteryLow, false);
});

function onBatteryLow(info) {
    alert("Battery Level Low " + info.level + "%");
}
"""""
```

The Critical Battery event

The Critical Battery event behaves similarly to the Battery Status event with the exception that the event is emitted only when the device reaches a critical battery threshold.

The event handler function receives the same parameters as the previous event so we could reuse the same function as for the Battery Status event if we are looking at battery changes and respond to the critical values of the battery; this usually starts with a level of 20 percent or less. It is good to know that 20 percent of battery charge is by no means a critical level. A battery charge below 10 percent is considered as dangerously low, a charge below 5 percent is a critical level, and a charge below 2 percent causes the system to automatically shut down immediately.

In the following example, I will show you how to present an alert dialog after the device reaches a critical battery level:

```
document.addEventListener("'deviceready"', function(event) {
    window.addEventListener("batterycritical", onBatteryCritical,
    false);
});

function onBatteryCritical(info) {
    alert("Battery Level Critical " + info.level + "%\nRecharge
    Soon!");
}
```

The following image shows a presented alert dialog after it has reached the critical battery level:

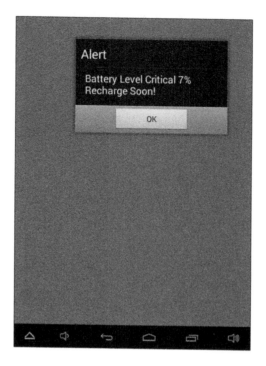

The Device Motion plugin

The Device plugin provides access to information about the device's accelerometer data. The accelerometer is a motion sensor that detects the change (delta) in movement relative to the current device orientation, in three dimensions along the x, y, and z axes.

Device Motion plugin is capturing accelerometer data at a specific snapshot in time. Values for the x, y, and z axes are expressed in m/s^2 and include the effect of gravity (9.81 m/s^2). For example, when the device is lying on top of the table and facing up, the x and y values are 0 and the z value is returning 9.81.

To install the plugin you need to run the following command:

```
phonegap plugin add cordova-plugin-device-motion
```

The Device Motion plugin has a few methods that return accelerometer data based on a real-time data representation of the sensor when we call these methods. The plugin provides access to methods through a global `navigator.accelerometer` object that is available after the `deviceready` event is fired; this is true for all other objects coming from PhoneGap plugins.

In the following example, I am going to print into the console the accelerometer object with data for all axes:

```
document.addEventListener("deviceready", onDeviceReady, false);
function onDeviceReady() {
    console.log(navigator.accelerometer);
}
```

The Device Motion plugin has the following methods available for use:

- `navigator.accelerometer.getCurrentAcceleration`
- `navigator.accelerometer.watchAcceleration`
- `navigator.accelerometer.clearWatch`

For this plugin, you need to run examples on the physical device since the emulator does not provide data for it out-of-the-box.

The getCurrentAcceleration method

The `getCurrentAcceleration` method is accessible through the `navigator.accelerometer.getCurrentAcceleration` method that returns the accelerator sensor data object back to the success callback function. It has four properties:

- `x`: Amount of acceleration on the x-axis
- `y`: Amount of acceleration on the y-axis
- `z`: Amount of acceleration on the z-axis
- `timestamp`: Creation timestamp in milliseconds

The method is defined as:

`navigator.accelerometer.getCurrentAcceleration(successCallback, errorCallback)`

You need to define at least a `successCallback` function that will receive the data. In the following example, we will show how to get the current acceleration data for the movement of the device:

```
function onSuccess(data) {
    var element = document.getElementById("phonegap"),
```

```
        response"";

    response = "'Acceleration X: "' + data.x + "'<br/>"' +
            "'Acceleration Y: "' + data.y + "'<br/>"' +
            "'Acceleration Z: "' + data.z + "'<br/>"' +
            "'Timestamp: "' + new Date(data.timestamp) +
            "'<br/>"';
    element.innerHTML = response;
}

function onError() {
    alert("'Error"');
};
document.addEventListener("'deviceready"', function(event) {
    navigator.accelerometer.getCurrentAcceleration(onSuccess,
        onError);
});
```

In the following screenshot, you can see the current acceleration values at the moment we request them:

watchAcceleration

The watchAcceleration method behaves similarly to the getCurrentAcceleration method. The only difference is that the callback functions are called at regular intervals until they are cancelled. The success callback method receives the same data that contains *x*, *y*, and *z* axis acceleration data. The method is defined as:

```
navigator.accelerometer.watchAcceleration(accelerometerSuccess,
accelerometerError, accelerometerOptions)
```

For the method you can set different intervals for sending acceleration data if you need it; the default value is 10,000. The value is expressed in milliseconds so, by default, new acceleration data is received every 10 seconds.

So the accelerometerOptions looks like: {frequency: 5000} if you want to receive updates every 5 seconds.

Another difference is that the watchAcceleration method returns a watch ID reference that you can use to stop listening in the future with the clearWatch method.

In the following screenshot, you can see the changes in acceleration when we change the device's position in space. The values are going to update in intervals, as defined:

```
function onSuccess(data) {
  var element = document.getElementById("phonegap");

  element.innerHTML += "'<p>Acceleration X: "' + data.x +
    "'<br/>"' + "'Acceleration Y: "' + data.y + "'<br/>"' +
      "'Acceleration Z: "' + data.z + "'<br/>"' +
        "'Timestamp: "' + new Date(data.timestamp) +
          "'<br/></p>"';
}

function onError() {
    alert("'Error"');
};

var options = { frequency: 3000 };  // Update every 3 seconds

document.addEventListener("'deviceready"', function(event) {
```

```
var watchID =
  navigator.accelerometer.watchAcceleration(onSuccess,
    onError, options);
});
```

Acceleration X: 0.15299999713897705
Acceleration Y: -0.15299999713897705
Acceleration Z: 9.807000160217285
Timestamp: Tue Jun 16 2015 00:01:03 GMT+0200 (CEST)

Acceleration X: 0.15299999713897705
Acceleration Y: -0.15299999713897705
Acceleration Z: 9.807000160217285
Timestamp: Tue Jun 16 2015 00:01:04 GMT+0200 (CEST)

Acceleration X: 0.15299999713897705
Acceleration Y: -0.15299999713897705
Acceleration Z: 9.652999877929688
Timestamp: Tue Jun 16 2015 00:01:05 GMT+0200 (CEST)

Acceleration X: -0.45899999141693115
Acceleration Y: 0.3059999942779541
Acceleration Z: 11.491999626159668
Timestamp: Tue Jun 16 2015 00:01:06 GMT+0200 (CEST)

Acceleration X: -6.742000102996826
Acceleration Y: 5.056000232696533
Acceleration Z: 4.13700008392334
Timestamp: Tue Jun 16 2015 00:01:07 GMT+0200 (CEST)

Acceleration X: -0.6119999885559082
Acceleration Y: 2.1449999809265137
Acceleration Z: 9.807000160217285
Timestamp: Tue Jun 16 2015 00:01:08 GMT+0200 (CEST)

Acceleration X: -0.9190000295639038
Acceleration Y: 1.0720000267028809
Acceleration Z: 9.347000122070312
Timestamp: Tue Jun 16 2015 00:01:09 GMT+0200 (CEST)

Acceleration X: -2.6040000915527344
Acceleration Y: -0.3059999942779541
Acceleration Z: 8.734000205993652
Timestamp: Tue Jun 16 2015 00:01:10 GMT+0200 (CEST)

Acceleration X: -7.660999774932861
Acceleration Y: 2.757999897003174
Acceleration Z: 6.129000186920166
Timestamp: Tue Jun 16 2015 00:01:11 GMT+0200 (CEST)

Acceleration X: -0.9190000295639038
Acceleration Y: 3.063999891281128
Acceleration Z: 9.807000160217285
Timestamp: Tue Jun 16 2015 00:01:12 GMT+0200 (CEST)

clearWatch

The `clearWatch` method stops watching for updates for the watch ID that we received after invoking the previous method:

`navigator.accelerometer.clearWatch(watchID);`

The parameter is as follows:

The `watchID` parameter is a valid watch ID received from the previous method invocation.

The Device Orientation plugin

The Device Orientation plugin has access to the device's compass. The compass acts as a sensor that displays the direction or heading that the device is pointed to; usually it is located on the top of the device. The compass sensor measures the heading in degrees from 0 to 359.99 degrees, where 0 denotes north.

To install the plugin, you need to run the following command:

`phonegap plugin add cordova-plugin-device-orientation`

The Device Orientation plugin provides a global `navigator.compass` object that is available only after the `deviceready` event is fired, so you need to listen for that event before doing any action or readings with the compass sensor:

```
document.addEventListener("deviceready", onDeviceReady, false);
function onDeviceReady() {
    console.log(navigator.compass);
}
```

The Device Orientation plugin has the following methods:

* `navigator.compass.getCurrentHeading`
* `navigator.compass.watchHeading`
* `navigator.compass.clearWatch`

With this plugin, you need to run examples on the physical device since the simulator does not provide data for it.

getCurrentHeading

The getCurrentHeading method returns the current compass heading. Heading data is returned via a CompassHeading object to a success callback function that contains much more information about the heading than we will show in the following example:

```
function onSuccess(heading) {
    alert("'Heading: "' + heading.magneticHeading);
};
function onError(error) {
    alert("'Heading: "' + heading.magneticHeading);
};
document.addEventListener("'deviceready"', function(event) {
  navigator.compass.getCurrentHeading(onSuccess, onError);
});
```

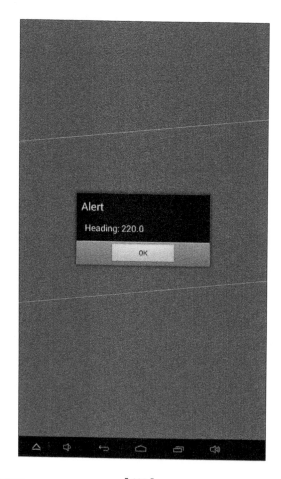

Heading object properties are:

- `magneticHeading`: The heading in degrees from 0 to 359.99 at a single moment in time.

- `trueHeading`: The heading relative to the geographic North pole in degrees 0 to 359.99 at a single moment in time. A negative value indicates that the true heading could not be determined.

- `headingAccuracy`: The deviation in degrees between the reported heading and the true heading.

- `timestamp`: The time at which this heading was determined.

watchHeading

The `watchHeading` method is similar to the first method. The only difference is that the callback functions are called at regular intervals until they are stopped. The success callback method receives the same data but it is updated based on the current state of the sensor. With every elapsed period, the success function is called.

Calling the `watchHeading` method will return a watch ID that you can later use to stop heading updates. The method has only a single value pair for the frequency: `{frequency:1000}`; this represents the period in milliseconds at which updates will occur.

In the following example, we are going to listen for heading updates:

```
function onSuccess(heading) {
    var element = document.getElementById('phonegap');
    element.innerHTML += "'<p>Heading: "' + heading.magneticHeading +
"'</p>"';
};

function onError(compassError) {
    alert("'Compass error: "' + compassError.code);
};

var options = {
    frequency: 3000
}; // Update every 3 seconds

document.addEventListener("'deviceready"', function(event) {
```

```
    var watchID = navigator.compass.watchHeading(onSuccess, onError,
options);
});
```

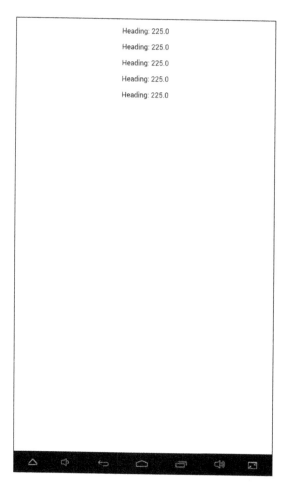

clearWatch

The `clearWatch` method stops watching for updates for the watch ID that we received after invoking the previous method. You can see it here:

```
navigator.compass.clearWatch(watchID);
```

The parameter is as follows:

The `watchID` parameter is a valid watch ID received from the previous method invocation.

The Geolocation plugin

The Geolocation plugin provides information about the device's location, identified with latitude and longitude. Most of the time, the device gets this information from **Global Positioning System** (**GPS**) or via network signals such as GSM/CDMA cell IDs, Wi-Fi, or Bluetooth MAC addresses. It's worth mentioning that, in addition to GPS, many new devices also have support for its competitor: GLONASS. Two positioning systems add more precision to location positioning.

In most scenarios, this plugin provides very accurate results that might differ depending on your location, whether you are outside or inside.

This plugin provides one of the most valuable sources of information for the application to manage data with. It can provide a user with local information or give the ability to search for various content located in the vicinity of the user. Most modern devices (even the cheapest) that have the latest version of their operating system usually have an embedded GPS module inside, so it will work on all of the devices without any problems.

To install the plugin, you need to run the following command:

```
phonegap plugin add org.apache.cordova.geolocation
```

This plugin defines a global `navigator.geolocation` object, at least for platforms where it is otherwise missing.

The Geolocation plugin has the following methods:

- `navigator.geolocation.getCurrentPosition`
- `navigator.geolocation.watchPosition`
- `navigator.geolocation.clearWatch`

With this plugin, the best way to run the examples is on the physical device. Another way is to use the simulator, mock the current location, and achieve the same effect.

getCurrentPosition

The `getCurrentPosition` method returns coordinates for the position of the device; it returns the `Position` object into a success callback function. Since the `Position` object contains many useful bits of information about the device's current location, it is explained in detail at the end of this chapter. Since there are many different factors involved in calculating the device's position (such as being indoors or trees blocking the sky), for the initial position data it can take up to 120 seconds to call the success callback function. The `getCurrentPosition` method is accessible as `navigator.geolocation.getCurrentPosition`:

```
navigator.geolocation.getCurrentPosition(geolocationSuccess,
                                        [geolocationError],
                                        [geolocationOptions]);
```

The parameters are as follows:

- `geolocationSuccess`: The success callback function that receives the current position
- `geolocationError`: The error callback function that is executed if an error occurs
- `geolocationOptions`: The geolocation options

The example code is as follows:

```
var onSuccess = function(position) {''
    alert("'Latitude: "' + position.coords.latitude + "'\n"' +
            "'Longitude: "' + position.coords.longitude + "'\n"' +
            "'Altitude: "' + position.coords.altitude + "'\n"' +
            "'Accuracy: "' + position.coords.accuracy + "'\n"' +
            "'Altitude Accuracy: "' +
              position.coords.altitudeAccuracy  + "'\n"' +
            "'Heading: "' + position.coords.heading + "'\n"' +
            "'Speed: "' + position.coords.speed + "'\n"' +
            "'Timestamp: "' + new Date(position.timestamp)  +
              "'\n"');
};

// onError Callback receives a PositionError object
//
function onError(error) {
    alert("'code: "' + error.code + "'\n"' +
            "'message: "' + error.message + "'\n"');
}
```

```
document.addEventListener('deviceready', function(event) {
  navigator.geolocation.getCurrentPosition(onSuccess, onError);
});
```

watchPosition

The watchPosition method is similar to getCurrentPosition except it updates periodically within the defined period. A success callback function receives the current position object as a parameter. The method returns a reference to the function as a watch ID, so it can be stopped in the future if there is a need to do that:

```
var watchId =
  navigator.geolocation.watchPosition(geolocationSuccess,
                                      [geolocationError],
                                      [geolocationOptions]);
```

The parameters are as follows:

- geolocationSuccess: The success callback function that passes the current position data
- geolocationError: The error callback function that executes if an error occurs
- geolocationOptions: The Additional geolocation options

The optional Geolocation parameter objects are as follows:

- enableHighAccuracy: A Boolean value that is true if we want to get results with the highest possible precision in the data for the location.

- timeout: The maximum length of time in milliseconds that is allowed to pass from the call to returning an update for the current location data; if it fails to do so in that time, it invokes an error callback function. It is worth noting that the first calculation of the position could take up to 120 seconds due to different circumstances (such as being inside a building or trees blocking the sky).

The example code is as follows:

```
// onSuccess Callback
//   This method accepts a `Position` object, which contains
//   the current GPS coordinates
//
var onSuccess = function(position) {
  var element = document.getElementById("phonegap"),
    response"";

  response += "'<p>Latitude: "' + position.coords.latitude +
    "'<br/>"';
  response += "'Longitude: "' + position.coords.longitude +
    "'<br/>"';
  response += "'Altitude: "' + position.coords.altitude +
    "'<br/>"';
  response += "'Accuracy: "' + position.coords.accuracy +
    "'<br/>"';
  response += "'Altitude Accuracy: "' +
    position.coords.altitudeAccuracy  + "'<br/>"';
  response += "'Heading: "' + position.coords.heading + "'<br/>"';
  response += "'Speed: "' + position.coords.speed + "'<br/>"';
  response += "'Timestamp: "' + new Date(position.timestamp) +
    "'<br/>"';
  response +=   "'</p>"';
  element.innerHTML += response;
};


// onError Callback receives a PositionError object
//
function onError(error) {
  alert("'code: "'    + error.code    + "'\n''message: "' +
    error.message'');
}
```

```
document.addEventListener("'deviceready"', function(event) {
  navigator.geolocation.watchPosition(onSuccess, onError, {
    timeout: 1000 });
});
```

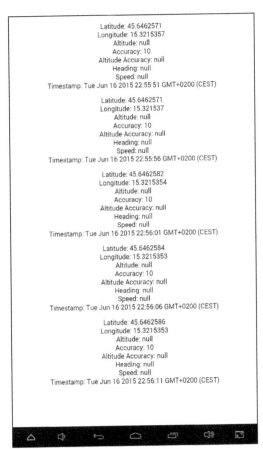

clearWatch

The `clearWatch` method stops watching for updates for the watch ID that we received after invoking the previous method for periodical updates for the current location:

```
navigator.geolocation.clearWatch(watchID);
```

The parameter is as follows:

The `watchID` parameter is a valid watch ID received from the previous method invocation.

The Position object

Since this is one of the most useful location-based sensors, I think we should get to know more about all the data that we receive when we are using this plugin.

Position is an object that is passed to a success callback function that contains coordinates and a timestamp created by the geolocation API. It has two properties to be called:

- coords: A set of geographic coordinates represented as a Coordinates object
- timestamp: The creation timestamp for coords

The Coordinates object

A Coordinates object is attached to a Position object that is available to callback functions in requests for the current position. It contains a set of properties that describe the geographic coordinates of a position. It has the following properties:

- latitude: Latitude in decimal degrees
- longitude: Longitude in decimal degrees
- altitude: Height of the position in meters above the ellipsoid
- accuracy: Accuracy level of the latitude and longitude coordinates in meters
- altitudeAccuracy: Accuracy level of the altitude coordinate in meters
- heading: Direction of travel, specified in degrees counting clockwise relative to true north
- speed: Current ground speed of the device, specified in meters per second

The Vibration plugin

The Vibration plugin provides access to the haptic motor that has been part of mobile devices since the invention of pagers, as they provide a discreet alert on updates that only you need to know. It provides a way to vibrate the device.

This is one of the plugins that you need to check regularly for changes since there is no complete support for all three major platforms and the features this plugin is providing. The iOS platform can only do one vibration at a time, while Android and Windows can do multiple vibrations in sequence. The plugin is defined as a global object through navigator.vibrate object.

To install the plugin, you need to run the following command:

```
phonegap plugin add cordova-plugin-vibration
```

The Vibration plugin provides a global `navigator.vibrate` object that is available only after the `deviceready` event is fired, so you need to listen for that event before performing an action or a pattern is emitted through the haptic motor

```
document.addEventListener("deviceready", onDeviceReady, false);
function onDeviceReady() {
    console.log(navigator.vibrate);
}
```

The Device Orientation plugin has the following method `navigator.vibrate`.

With this plugin, you need to run examples on the physical device since the simulator does not provide data for it.

This is a plugin that you cannot see so you need to physically touch your device to feel the vibration working.

Vibrate

The `Vibrate` method is the most common one and has three different functionalities based on parameters passed to it on how to behave.

Standard vibrate

It vibrates for a given amount of time, specified in milliseconds. You can see this in the following example:

```
navigator.vibrate(duration);
```

The example code is as follows:

```
document.addEventListener("'deviceready"', function(event) {
    navigator.vibrate(1000); // vibrates for one second
});
```

Vibrating with a pattern (Android and Windows only)

It vibrates with a specific pattern that is provided by the method. You need to provide a sequence of durations (in milliseconds) at which to turn on or off the vibrator. You can see this below:

```
navigator.vibrate(pattern);
```

The following example shows the vibrating sequence:

```
document.addEventListener("'deviceready"', function(event) {
  // Vibrate for 1 second
  // Wait for 1 second
  // Vibrate for 3 seconds
  // Wait for 1 second
  // Vibrate for 5 seconds
  navigator.vibrate([1000, 1000, 3000, 1000, 5000]);
});
```

Cancelling the vibration (not supported in iOS)

This immediately cancels any currently running vibration:

```
navigator.vibrate(0);
```

Passing in a parameter of 0, an empty array, or an array with one element of value 0 will cancel any vibrations.

Summary

In this chapter, we familiarized ourselves with advanced plugins that give the ability to receive data from sensors or listen for them in a specific period of time. These sensors are available in the most of the latest devices for all three most popular mobile platforms.

As we can see from the examples, these plugins provide a powerful interface between the native hardware API and any hybrid mobile application that we want to build.

In the next chapter, we will be covering how to access native camera capabilities and access existing media files to be used inside our application.

7
Accessing Media Content

This chapter will cover how to access native camera capabilities and existing media files that are to be used inside the application. We will cover selected media plugins for the native features that are available for PhoneGap.

- File Transfer
- Contacts
- Camera
- InApp Browser

Introducing multimedia

In the world of fast Internet connections and powerful devices in your pocket, the need for multimedia content is rising. You need to have a way to enrich it by accessing the various recording capabilities of the device—for instance, the camera for photos and movies, or the microphone for recording audio.

Media

One of the most used features on a mobile device is the ability to take photos on the camera; almost all applications require some kind of photo upload facility, ranging from setting profile pictures to embedding photos into posts.

File management

Another problem that most applications face is the need to store content that has been created or downloaded. For example, HTML5 supports a persistent storage API for local storage but it has some limitations. With plugins for file transfer, we can download or upload files in the background without affecting the main thread of the application. The possibilities are endless and we do not need to rely on native applications for them.

I am using an Android device for the following examples, but, since they work on all platforms, you can try them with other platforms too. You need to pay special attention to the fact that some devices have development mode disabled by default; thus, please search online for how to enable development mode for your device since the procedure differs by model.

Contacts

Many applications try to spread their message as quickly as possible but this isn't possible unless there is a way to share with the user's friends. Here, the Contacts plugin gives you the ability to access all of the user's contacts via a single method. You can also create or update existing contacts, if you need to.

File Transfer

The File Transfer plugin enables you to download uploaded files from your server. It is used together with media content capability to upload to your server without interrupting your main thread. File Transfer provides a way to upload HTTP multi-part POST requests.

To install the plugin, you need to run the following command:

```
phonegap plugin add cordova-plugin-file-transfer
```

The File Transfer plugin will make available two global objects—`FileTransfer` and `FileUploadOptions`—that will be available after the `deviceready` event has been fired. We are going to describe them in detail in the following paragraphs:

```
document.addEventListener("deviceready", function() {
    console.log(FileTransfer);
}, false);
```

Examples for this plugin need to have the server to communicate with. Since the scope of this book is limited to learning PhoneGap essentials, I am going to show you how it works with real code, however, since you do not have a running server, you cannot run this on your devices.

The FileTransfer object

The FileTransfer object provides a way to upload files using an HTTP multi-part POST request, and to download files as well. The process is running in the background so there is no slowdown of the main thread when downloading or uploading files.

The property is as follows:

- onprogress: This is called with a ProgressEvent whenever a new chunk of data is transferred

The methods are as follows:

- upload: Sends a file to a server
- download: Downloads a file from a server
- abort: Aborts an in-progress transfer

The FileUploadResult object

A FileUploadResult object is passed to the success callback of the FileTransfer object's upload() method and contains all the information you need in order to check whether the upload was successful.

The properties are as follows:

- bytesSent: The number of bytes sent to the server as part of the upload
- responseCode: The HTTP response code returned by the server
- response: The HTTP response returned by the server
- headers: The HTTP response headers returned by the server

Upload

The Upload function of the FileTransfer object uploads any kind of file to your remote server.

The parameters are as follows:

- fileURL: Filesystem URL representing the file on the device. For backwards-compatibility, this can also be the full path of the file on the device.
- server: URL of the server to receive the file, as encoded by encodeURI().

- **successCallback**: A callback function that is passed a `FileUploadResult` object.

- **errorCallback**: A callback function that executes if an error occurs retrieving the `FileUploadResult`. Invoked with a `FileTransferError` object.

Here is an example:

```
// fileURL path is a valid and available path for this application
var fileURL = "cdvfile://localhost/persistent/path/to/profile-photo.
png",
  uri = encodeURI ("http://www.myserver.com/profile-picture");

var onSuccess = function(entry) {
    var element = document.getElementById("phonegap"),
      response = "";

  response += "Code = " + entry.responseCode + "\n";
  response += "Response = " + entry.response + "\n";
  response += "Sent = " + entry.bytesSent + "\n";
  element.innerHTML += response;
};

var onError = function(error) {
  alert("download error\n source " + error.source + "\n" +
      "target " + error.target + "\n" +
      "error code" + error.code);
};

document.addEventListener("deviceready", function(event) {
  var options = new FileUploadOptions();
  options.fileKey= "file";
  options.fileName= fileURL.substr(fileURL.lastIndexOf("/") + 1);
  options.mimeType= "image/png";
  options.params = {
    username: "username"
  };

  var fileTransfer = new FileTransfer();
  fileTransfer.upload(fileURL, uri, onSuccess, onError, options);
});
```

Download

The FileTransfer download function downloads files from the remote server:

```
download (source, target, successCallback, errorCallback, options)
```

The parameters are as follows:

- source: URL of the server to download the file, as encoded by encodeURI().
- target: Filesystem URL representing the file on the device.
- successCallback: A callback function that is passed a FileEntry object.
- errorCallback: A callback function that executes if an error occurs when retrieving the FileEntry. Invoked with a FileTransferError object.
- options: Optional parameters, currently only supports headers. Useful for sending authorization details or authorization tokens.

Here is an example:

```
// fileURL path is a valid and available path for this application
var fileURL = "cdvfile://localhost/persistent/path/to/downloads/",
    uri = encodeURI("http://www.myserver.com/profile-picture"),
    options = {
      headers: {
        "Authorization": "Basic fdgsdfgsdfhgjdfshgsdfgdjf=="
      }
    };

var onSuccess = function(entry) {
  var element = document.getElementById("phonegap"),
      response = "";

  response = "download complete: " + entry.toURL();
  element.innerHTML += response;
};

var onError = function(error) {
  alert("download error\n source " + error.source + "\n" +
        "target " + error.target + "\n" +
        "error code" + error.code);
};

document.addEventListener("deviceready", function(event) {
    var fileTransfer = new FileTransfer();
    fileTransfer.download(uri, fileURL, onSuccess, onError, options);
});
```

Abort

The Abort function aborts an in-progress file transfer. The `onError` callback function is passed a `FileTransferError` object.

Here is an example:

```
// fileURL path is a valid and available path for this application
var fileURL = "cdvfile://localhost/persistent/path/to/profile-photo.
png",
        uri = encodeURI("http://www.myserver.com/profile-picture");

var onSuccess = function(entry) {
  alert("Should not be called");
};

var onError = function(error) {
  alert("download error\n source " + error.source + "\n" +
        "target " + error.target + "\n" +
        "error code" + error.code);
};

document.addEventListener("deviceready", function(event) {
  var options = new FileUploadOptions();
  options.fileKey="file";
  options.fileName="profile-picture.png";
  options.mimeType="image/png";

  var fileTransfer = new FileTransfer();
  fileTransfer.upload(fileURL, uri, onSuccess, onError, options);
  fileTransfer.abort();
});
```

Contacts

The Contacts plugin is one of the most useful features if you are trying to build an application for a social platform. It can have advantages when it comes to making a decision about native applications; many other features are available for web applications directly through HTML5 technologies, and this one requires PhoneGap to make it work.

To install the plugin, you need to run the following command:

```
phonegap plugin add cordova-plugin-contacts
```

With this plugin, you need to run examples on the physical device since the simulator does not provide data for it.

This plugin defines a global `navigator.contacts` object that provides access to the device contacts; it is available after the `deviceready` event has been fired:

```
document.addEventListener("deviceready", onDeviceReady, false);
function onDeviceReady() {
    console.log(navigator.contacts);
}
```

The Contacts plugin has the following methods:

- `navigator.contacts.create`
- `navigator.contacts.find`
- `navigator.contacts.pickContact`

Contact

The Contacts plugin is one of the few plugins for which we are going to cover every specific object required. This plugin is recommended to understand the format of the objects we are receiving and also to create new contacts. So let's go over the objects you should know before covering other useful methods.

The Contact object

The `Contact` object represents a user's contact. Within the context of the Contacts plugin, the `Contact` object can be created, stored, or removed from the device's contacts database. Contacts can also be retrieved from the database by invoking the `navigator.contacts.find` method, which we are going to learn about in the following sections, with accompanying examples.

The properties are as follows:

- `id`: A globally unique identifier
- `displayName`: The name of this Contact, suitable for displaying to end users
- `name`: An object containing all the components of a person's name
- `nickname`: A casual name by which to address the contact
- `phoneNumbers`: An array of all the contact's phone numbers
- `emails`: An array of all the contact's e-mail addresses
- `addresses`: An array of all the contact's addresses
- `ims`: An array of all the contact's IM addresses

- organizations: An array of all the contact's organizations

- birthday: The birthday of the contact

- note: A note about the contact

- photos: An array of the contact's photos

- categories: An array of all the user-defined categories associated with the contact

- urls: An array of web pages associated with the contact

The methods are as follows:

- clone: Returns a new Contact object that is a deep copy of the calling object, with the ID property set to null

- remove: Removes the contact from the device's contacts database, otherwise it executes an error callback with a ContactError object

- save: Saves a new contact to the device's contacts database, or updates an existing contact if a contact with the same ID already exists

ContactName

This contains different kinds of information about a Contact object's name.

The properties are as follows:

- formatted: The complete name of the contact (DOMString)
- familyName: The contact's family name (DOMString)
- givenName: The contact's given name (DOMString)
- middleName: The contact's middle name (DOMString)
- honorificPrefix: The contact's prefix (For example, Mr. or Dr.) (DOMString)
- honorificSuffix: The contact's suffix (For example, Esq.) (DOMString)

ContactField

The ContactField object is a reusable component that represents the contact fields generically. Each ContactField object contains a value, type, and pref property. A Contact object stores several properties in ContactField[] arrays, such as phone numbers and email addresses.

In most instances, there are no predetermined values for a ContactField object's type attribute. For example, a phone number can specify type values of home, work, mobile, iPhone, or any other value that is supported by a particular device platform's contact database.

The properties are as follows:

- `type`: A string that indicates what type of field this is—home, for example (DOMString)
- `value`: The value of the field, such as a phone number or email address (DOMString)
- `pref`: Set to true if this `ContactField` contains the user's preferred value (Boolean)

ContactAddress

The `ContactAddress` object stores the properties of a single address of a contact. A Contact object may include more than one address in a `ContactAddress[]` array.

The properties are as follows:

- `pref`: Set to true if this `ContactAddress` contains the user's preferred value (Boolean)
- `type`: A string indicating what type of field this is, home for example (DOMString)
- `formatted`: The full address formatted for display (DOMString)
- `streetAddress`: The full street address (DOMString)
- `locality`: The city or locality (DOMString)
- `region`: The state or region (DOMString)
- `postalCode`: The zip code or postal code (DOMString)
- `country`: The country name (DOMString)

ContactOrganization

The `ContactOrganization` object stores a contact's organization properties. A `Contactobject` stores one or more `ContactOrganization` objects in an array.

The properties are as follows:

- `pref`: Set to true if this ContactOrganization contains the user's preferred value (Boolean)
- `type`: A string that indicates what type of field this is—home, for example _(DOMString)
- `name`: The name of the organization (DOMString)
- `department`: The department the contact works for (DOMString)
- `title`: The contact's title at the organization (DOMString)

The create method

The `create` method creates a new `Contact` object that is not yet saved into the contacts database. So you need to execute the save method on this `Contact` object to save it persistently in the database.

Here is an example:

```
var onSuccess = function(contact) {
  var element = document.getElementById("phonegap"),
    response;

  response += "<b>New contact is created</b> <br/>";
  response += "First name: " + contact.name.givenName + "<br/>";
  response += "Family name " + contact.name.familyName + "<br/>";
  element.innerHTML += response;
};

var onError = function(error) {
  alert("Error = " + error.code);
};

document.addEventListener("deviceready", function(event) {
  var contact = navigator.contacts.create();
  contact.displayName = "Mike";
  contact.nickname = contact.displayName; // we need both to support
all devices

  var phoneNumbers = [];
  phoneNumbers.push(new ContactField("work", "212-555-1234", false));
  phoneNumbers.push(new ContactField("mobile", "917-555-5432", true));
// default number
  contact.phoneNumbers = phoneNumbers;

  // populate some fields
  var name = new ContactName();
  name.givenName = "Michael";
  name.familyName = "Smith";
  contact.name = name;

  contact.save(onSuccess, onError);
});
```

In the following screenshot, you should see a response text after a new contact has been successfully created:

Find

The find method executes asynchronously, querying the device's contacts database and returning an array of Contact objects. The resulting objects are passed to the contactSuccess callback function specified by the contactSuccess parameter.

The contactFields parameter specifies the fields to be used as a search qualifier. A contactFields value of * searches all contact fields. The contactFindOptions. filter string can be used as a search filter when querying the contacts database. If provided, a case-insensitive, partial value match is applied to each field specified in the contactFields parameter. If there's a match for any of the specified fields, the contact is returned. Use the contactFindOptions.desiredFields parameter to control which contact properties must be returned back.

The parameters are as follows:

- contactFields: Contact fields to use as a search qualifier
- contactSuccess: Success callback function invoked with the array of Contact objects returned from the database
- contactError: Error callback function, invoked when an error occurs
- contactFindOptions: Search options to filter navigator.contacts

The keys include:

- filter: The search string used to find navigator.contacts.
- multiple: Determines if the find operation returns multiple navigator.contacts.
- desiredFields: Contact fields to be returned back. If specified, the resulting Contact object only features values for these fields.

Here is an example:

```javascript
var onSuccess = function(contacts) {
  var element = document.getElementById("phonegap"),
    response;

  for (var i = 0; i < contacts.length; i++) {
    response += "<p>First name: " + contacts[i].name.givenName +
"<br/>";
    response += "Family name " + contacts[i].name.familyName + "</p>";
  }
  element.innerHTML += response;
};

var onError = function(error) {
  alert("Error = " + error);
};

document.addEventListener("deviceready", function(event) {
```

```
    var filter = ["displayName", "name"];

    var options = new ContactFindOptions();
    options.filter = "";
    options.multiple = true;

    navigator.contacts.find(filter, onSuccess, onError, options);
});
```

After running the example code, you should see the newly created contact on the list. If you are running the example on your device, you should see your contacts too:

First name: Michael
Family name Smith

pickContact

The `navigator.contacts.pickContact` method launches the contact picker to select a single contact. The resulting object is passed to the `contactSuccess` callback function specified by the `contactSuccess` parameter.

The parameters are as follows:

- `contactSuccess`: Success callback function invoked with a single `Contact` object
- `contactError`: Error callback function, invoked when an error occurs

The following example shows how to choose a contact and then show it on the screen:

```
navigator.contacts.pickContact(function(contact){
    console.log("The following contact has been selected: " + JSON.
stringify(contact));
}, function(err){
    console.log("Error: " + err);
});
```

If you run the example, you should see the following contact picker from which to select one contact:

After selecting a contact, you should be able to see a response similar to the one shown in the following screenshot:

Camera

The Camera plugin is one of the most useful features available through PhoneGap as it can access native UI components to take photos or select photos from the image library. Photos are present in many applications—for example, they can be used as profile pictures. This is one of the most used plugins for PhoneGap.

To install the plugin, you need to run the following command:

```
phonegap plugin add cordova-plugin-camera
```

The Camera plugin defines a global `navigator.camera` object, which provides an API for taking pictures and for choosing images from the system's image library. The object is available only after the `deviceready` event has been fired:

```
document.addEventListener("deviceready", onDeviceReady, false);
function onDeviceReady() {
    console.log(navigator.camera);
}
```

The Camera plugin has the following method:

- `navigator.camera.getPicture`

The received image data can be displayed inside the application, saved to the application file directories, or used to send the image to the server.

getPicture

This takes a photo using the camera, or retrieves a photo from the device's image gallery. The image is passed to the success callback as a base64-encoded string, or as the URI for the image file. The method itself returns a `CameraPopoverHandle` object that can be used to reposition the file selection pop-over.

This function opens the default camera application to take photos or select existing ones. Once you take the photo, the camera application closes and the `onSuccess` callback function is called:

`navigator.camera.getPicture(onSuccess, onError, options);`

The parameters are as follows:

- `onSuccess`: A success callback function that returns image data. Depending on the camera options, it returns a base64-encoded photo or the path to the image file location.

- `onError`: An error callback function.

- `options`: Additional options for setting up the camera specifications.

    ○ `quality`: Quality of the saved image, expressed in the range 0-100, where 100 is typically full resolution with no loss from file compression. The default is 50.

    ○ `destinationType`: Chooses the format of the return value. The default is FILEURI. There are two available options:

    `Camera.DestinationType.DATA_URL`: Returns the image as a base64-encoded string.

`Camera.DestinationType.FILE_URI`: return image as file URI:

- ○ `sourceType`: Sets the source of the picture. The default is CAMERA.

  `Camera.PictureSourceType.CAMERA`: Opens the camera application.

  `Camera.PictureSourceType. PHOTOLIBRARY`: Opens the photo library:

- ○ `allowEdit`: Allows simple editing of an image before selection.

- ○ `encodingType`: Chooses the returned image file's encoding. The default is JPEG.

  `Camera.EncodingType.JPEG`

  `Camera.EncodingType.PNG`:

- ○ `targetWidth`: Width in pixels to scale the image. Must be used with `targetHeight`. Aspect ratio remains constant.

- ○ `targetHeight`: Height in pixels to scale the image. Must be used with `targetWidth`. Aspect ratio remains constant.

- ○ `mediaType`: Sets the type of media to select from. Only works when `PictureSourceType` is PHOTOLIBRARY.

  `Camera.MediaType.PICTURE`: Shows only pictures.

  `Camera.MediaType.VIDEO`: Shows only videos.

  `Camera.MediaType.ALLMEDIA`: Shows all media:

- ○ `correctOrientation`: Rotates the image to correct for the orientation of the device during capture.

- ○ `saveToPhotoAlbum`: Save the image to the photo album on the device after capture.

- ○ `cameraDirection`: Chooses the camera to use (front- or back-facing). The default is BACK:

  `Camera.Direction.BACK`: Back-facing camera

  `Camera.Direction.FRONT`: Front-facing camera

Here is an example:

```
var onSuccess = function(imageData) {
  var element = document.getElementById("phonegap"),
      image = document.createElement("img");

  image.src = imageData;
  image.setAttribute("width", "100%");
```

```
      element.appendChild(image);
  };

  var onError = function(error) {
    alert("Error = " + error);
  };

  document.addEventListener("deviceready", function(event) {
    var options = {
      quality: 50,
      destinationType: Camera.DestinationType.FILE_URI,
      sourceType : Camera.PictureSourceType.CAMERA,
      allowEdit : false,
      encodingType: Camera.EncodingType.JPEG,
      saveToPhotoAlbum: false
    };

    navigator.camera.getPicture(onSuccess, onError, options);
  });
```

The following image shows the screen for taking photos, using the default image-taking service on your device:

When we take the photo, our application receives the photo data object ready to display on the screen. The following image shows the photo we have just taken:

cleanup

The `cleanup` method is used to remove photos from temporary storage, so they no longer take up space on the camera. It is only used when you take new photos and they are accessed from storage and not from memory. This method is defined as:

```
navigator.camera.cleanup( cameraSuccess, cameraError );
```

You should implement the success function to receive it when it is successfully cleared:

```
function onSuccess() {
    console.log("Camera cleanup success.")
}


function onFail(message) {
    alert("Failed because: " + message);
}
document.addEventListener("deviceready", function(event) {
navigator.camera.cleanup(onSuccess, onFail);
});
```

InAppBrowser

The InAppBrowser plugin allows you to open regular web pages inside your application without the need to open an external browser application. This is useful for opening pages for external authentication with social accounts, or for accessing third-party web pages.

The InAppBrowser is recommended if you need to load third-party (untrusted) content, instead of loading it into the main Cordova WebView. The InAppBrowser is not subject to a whitelist, nor does it open links in the system browser.

To install the plugin, you need to run the following command:

```
phonegap plugin add org.apache.cordova.inappbrowser
```

The InAppBrowser window behaves like a regular web browser; thus, it cannot access any PhoneGap native APIs. Inside InAppBrowser, you can only use those HTML5 features that are available for regular web apps; they can provide the same or (similar) behavior. The plugin provides a simple UI with Back, Forward, and Done controls, which can be hidden too:

```
var ref = window.open("http://www.google.com", "_blank",
    "location=yes");
```

This plugin replaces window.open in the global scope, but InAppBrowser is not available until after the deviceready event has been fired. If you want to open the web page in the default device's web browser, you can do that too by setting the target to _system instead of _blank:

```
document.addEventListener("deviceready", onDeviceReady, false);
function onDeviceReady() {
    console.log("window.open works well");
}
```

The InAppBrowser object

The InAppBrowser object is returned from a call to window.open and provides a reference to the window currently opened.

The methods are as follows:

- addEventListener: Adds an event listener for an event from InAppBrowser. There are four events available (loadstart, loadend, loaderror, and exit). The callback function receives an InAppBrowser event object.
- removeEventListener: Removes the listener for a specific event.
- close: Closes the window with the browser opened.

The InAppBrowserEvent object

This is an object the event listener sends to the callback function.

The properties are as follows:

- type: The eventname, that is, loadstart, loadstop, loaderror, or exit
- url: The URL that was loaded
- code: The error code, only in the case of loaderror
- message: The error message, only in the case of loaderror

Open

This opens an URL in a new InAppBrowser instance, the current browser instance, or the system browser:

```
var ref = window.open(url, target, options);
```

The parameters are as follows:

- ref: Reference to the InAppBrowser window.
- url: The URL to load. Call encodeURI() on this if the URL contains Unicode characters.
- target: The target in which to load the URL—an optional parameter that defaults to _self:
    - _self: Opens in Cordova WebView if the URL is in the whitelist; otherwise it opens in the InAppBrowser
    - _blank: Opens in the InAppBrowser
    - _system: Opens in the system's web browser

- `options`: Options for the InAppBrowser:
  - ° `location`: Set to `Yes` or `No` to turn the InAppBrowser's location bar on or off.

Here is an example:

```
document.addEventListener("deviceready", function(event) {
  var ref = window.open("http://www.google.com", "_blank",
"location=yes");
  ref.addEventListener("loadstop", function(event) {
   alert("Loaded " + event.url);
  });
});
```

Summary

In this chapter, we went through the basics of accessing media content and creating new content. As we saw from the examples, PhoneGap plugins simplify and streamline the process of accessing media that, without it, would be inaccessible.

Now you can create hybrid mobile applications that need to take photos, access media content, and save data needed for offline use inside the application.

8
Application Development Workflow

This chapter will cover some of the basics on how to work with the PhoneGap application development and how to start building the application. We will go over some useful steps and tips to get the most out of your PhoneGap application. In this chapter, you will learn the following topics:

- An introduction to a development workflow
- Best practices
- Testing
- Debugging
- User interfaces

An introduction to a development workflow

PhoneGap solves a great problem of developing mobile applications for multiple platforms at the same time, but still it is pretty much open about how you want to approach the creation of an application. You do not have any predefined frameworks that come out of-the-box by default. It just allows you to use the standard web technologies such as the HTML5, CSS3, and JavaScript languages for hybrid mobile application development. The applications are executed in wrappers that are custom-built to work on every platform and the underlying web view behaves in the same way on all the platforms. For accessing device APIs, it relies on the standard API bindings to access every device's sensors or the other features.

The developers who start using PhoneGap usually come from different backgrounds, as shown in the following list:

- Mobile developers who want to expand the functionality of their application on other platforms but do not want to learn a new language for each platform

- Web developers who want to port their existing desktop web application to a mobile application; if they are using a responsive design, it is quite simple to do this

- Experienced mobile developers who want to use both the native and web components in their application, so that the web components can communicate with the internal native application code as well

The PhoneGap project itself is pretty simple. By default, it can open an `index.html` page and load the initial CSS file, JavaScript, and other resources needed to run it. Besides the user's resources, it needs to refer the `cordova.js` file, which provides the API bindings for all the plugins. From here onwards, you can take different steps but usually the process falls in two main workflows: web development workflow and native platform development.

Web project development

A web project development workflow can be used when you want to create a PhoneGap application that runs on many mobile operating systems with as little as possible changes to a specific one. So there is a single codebase that is working along with all the different devices. It has become possible with the latest versions since the introduction of the **command-line interface** (CLI). This automates the tedious work involved in a lot of the functionalities while taking care of each platform, such as building the app, copying the web assets in the correct location for every supported platform, adding platform-specific changes, and finally running build scripts to generate binaries.

This process can be automated even more with build system automating tasks such as Gulp or Grunt. You can run these tasks before running PhoneGap commands. This way you can optimize the assets before they are used. Also you can run JSLint automatically for any change or doing automatic builds for every platform that is available. Unfortunately, information about these techniques or services is far beyond the scope of this book and that's why they're only mentioned. You will need to seek more information about them in other books or from the Internet.

Native platform development

A native platform development workflow can be imagined as a focus on building an application for a single platform and the need to change the lower-level platform details. The benefit of using this approach is that it gives you more flexibility and you can mix the native code with a WebView code and impose communication between them. This is appropriate for those functionalities that contain a section of the features that are not hard to reproduce with web views only; for example, a video app where you can do the video editing in the native code and all the social features and interaction can be done with web views.

Even if you want to start with this approach, it is better to start the new project as a web project development workflow and then continue to separate the code for your specific needs. One thing to keep in mind is that, to develop with this approach, it is better to develop the application in more advanced IDE environments, which you would usually use for building native applications.

Best practices

The running of hybrid mobile applications requires some sacrifices in terms of performance and functionality; so it is good to go over some useful tips for new PhoneGap developers.

Use local assets for the UI

As mobile devices are limited by the connection speeds and mobile data plans are not generous with the bandwidth, you need to prepare all the UI components in the application before deploying to the app store. Nobody will want to use an application that takes a few seconds to load the server-rendered UI when the same thing could be done on the client. For example, the Google Fonts or other non-UI assets that are usually loaded from the server for the web applications are good enough as for the development process, but for the production; you need to store all the assets in the application's container and not download them during its run process. You do not want the application to wait while an important part is being loaded.

The best advice on the UI that I can give you is to adopt the **Single Page Application (SPA)** design; it is a client-side application that is run from one request from a web page. Initial loading means taking care of loading all the assets that are required for the application in order to function, and any further updates are done via AJAX (such as loading data). When you use SPA, not only do you minimize the amount of interaction with the server, you also organize your application in a more efficient manner. One of the benefits is that the application doesn't need to wait for every `deviceready` event for each additional page that it loads from the start.

Network access for data

As you have seen in the previous section, there are many limitations that mobile applications face with the network connection—from mobile data plans to the network latency. So you do not want it to rely on the crucial elements, unless real-time communication is required for the application. Try to keep the network access only to access crucial data and everything else that is used frequently can be packed into assets.

If the received data does not change often, it is advisable to cache it for offline use. There are many ways to achieve this, such as `localStorage`, `sessionStorage`, `WebSQL`, or a `file`. When loading data, try to load only the data you need at that moment. If you have a comment section, it will make sense if you load all thousand comments; the first twenty comments should be enough to start with.

Non-blocking UI

When you are loading additional data to show in the application, don't try to pause the application until you receive all the data that you need. You can add some animation or a spinner to show the progress. Do not let the user stare at the same screen when he presses the button. Try to disable the actions once they are in motion in order to prevent sending the same action multiple times.

CSS animations

As most of the modern mobile platforms now support CSS3 with a more or less consistent feature set, it is better to make the animations and transitions with CSS rather than with the plain JavaScript DOM manipulation, which was done before CSS3. CSS3 is much faster as the browser engine supports the hardware acceleration of CSS animations and is more fluid than the JavaScript animations. CSS3 supports translations and full keyframe animations as well, so you can be really creative in making your application more interactive.

Click events

You should avoid click events at any cost and use only touch events. They work in the same way as they do in the desktop browser. They take a longer time to process as the mobile browser engine needs to process the `touch` or `touchhold` events before firing a click event. This usually takes 300 ms, which is more than enough to give an additional impression of slow responses. So try to start using `touchstart` or `touchend` events. There is a solution for this called `FastClick.js`. It is a simple, easy-to-use library for eliminating the 300 ms delay between a physical tap and the firing of a click event on mobile browsers.

Performance

The performance that we get on the desktops isn't reflected in mobile devices. Most of the developers assume that the performance doesn't change a lot, especially as most of them test the applications on the latest mobile devices and a vast majority of the users use mobile devices that are 2-3 years old. You have to keep in mind that even the latest mobile devices have a slower CPU, less RAM, and a weaker GPU. Recently, mobile devices are catching up in the sheer numbers of these components but, in reality, they are slower and the maximum performance is limited due to the battery life that prevents it from using the maximum performance for a prolonged time.

Optimize the image assets

We are not limited any more by the app size that we need to deploy. However, you need to optimize the assets, especially images, as they take a large part of the assets, and make them appropriate for the device. You should prepare images in the right size; do not add the biggest size of the image that you have and force the mobile device to scale the image in HTML. Choosing the right image size is not an easy task if you are developing an application that should support a wide array of screens, especially for Android that has a very fragmented market with different screen sizes. The scaled images might have additional artifacts on the screen and they might not look so crisp. You will be hogging additional memory just for an image that could leave a smaller memory footprint. You should remember that mobile devices still have limited resources and the battery doesn't last forever.

If you are going to use PhoneGap Build, you will need to make sure you do not exceed the limit as the service still has a limited size.

Offline status

As we all know, the network access is slow and limited, but the network coverage is not perfect so it is quite possible that your application will be working in the offline mode even in the usual locations. Bad reception can be caused by being inside a building with thick walls or in the basement. Some weather conditions can affect the reception too. The application should be able to handle this situation and respond to it properly, such as by limiting the parts of the application that require a network connection or caching data and syncing it when you are online once again. This is one of the aspects that developers usually forget to test in the offline mode to see how the app behaves under certain conditions. You should have a plugin available in order to detect the current state and the events when it passes between these two modes.

Load only what you need

There are a lot of developers that do this, including myself. We need some part of the library or a widget from a framework, which we don't need for anything other than this, and yet we are a bit lazy about loading a specific element and the full framework. This can load an immense amount of resources that we will never need but they will still run in the background. It might also be the root cause of some of the problems as some libraries do not mix well and we can spend hours trying to solve this problem.

Transparency

You should try to use as little as possible of the elements that have transparent parts as they are quite processor-intensive because you need to update screen on every change behind them. The same things apply to the other visual elements that are processor-intensive such as shadows or gradients. The great thing is that all the major platforms have moved away from flashy graphical elements and started using the flat UI design.

JSHint

If you use JSHint throughout the development, it will save you a lot of time when developing things in JavaScript. It is a static code analysis tool for checking whether the JavaScript source code complies with the coding rules. It will detect all the common mistakes done with JavaScript, as JavaScript is not a compiled language and you can't see the error until you run the code. At the same time, JSHint can be a very restrictive and demanding tool. Many beginners in JavaScript, PhoneGap, or mobile programming could be overwhelmed with the number of errors or bad practices that JSHint will point out.

Testing

The testing of applications is an important aspect of build applications, and mobile applications are no exception. With a slight difference for most of the development that doesn't require native device APIs, you can use the platform simulators and see the results. However, if you are using the native device APIs that are not supported through simulators, then you need to have a real device in order to run a test on it.

It is not unusual to use desktop browsers resized to mobile device screen resolution to emulate their screen while you are developing the application just to test the UI screens, since it is much faster and easier than building and running the application on a simulator or real device for every small change. There is a great plugin for the Google Chrome browser called Apache Ripple. It can be run without any additional tools. The Apache Ripple simulator runs as a web app in the Google Chrome browser. In Cordova, it can be used to simulate your app on a number of iOS and Android devices and it provides basic support for the core Cordova plugins such as Geolocation and Device Orientation. You can run the application in a real device browser or use the PhoneGap developer app. This simplifies the workflow as you can test the application on your mobile device without the need to re-sign, recompile, or reinstall your application to test the code. The only disadvantage is that with simulators, you cannot access the device APIs that aren't available in the regular web browsers. The PhoneGap developer app allows you to access device APIs as long as you are using one of the supplied APIs.

It is good if you remember to always test the application on real devices at least before deploying to the app store. Computers have almost unlimited resources as compared to mobile devices, so the application that runs flawlessly on the computer might fail on mobile devices due to low memory.

As simulators are faster than the real device, you might get the impression that it will work on every device equally fast, but it won't—especially with older devices. So, if you have an older device, it is better to test the response on it.

Another reason to use the mobile device instead of the simulator is that it is hard to get a good usability experience from clicking on the interface on the computer screen without your fingers interfering and blocking the view on the device.

Even though it is rare that you would get some bugs with the plain PhoneGap that was introduced with the new version, it might still happen. If you use the UI framework, it is good if you try it on the different versions of the operating systems as they might not work flawlessly on each of them. Even though hybrid mobile application development has been available for some time, it is still evolving, and as yet there are no default UI frameworks to use. Even the PhoneGap itself is still evolving.

As with the UI, the same thing applies to the different plugins. Some of the features might get deprecated or might not be supported, so it is good if you implement alternatives or give feedback to the users about why this will not work. From experience, the average PhoneGap application will use at least ten plugins or different libraries for the final deployment. Every additional plugin or library installed can cause conflicts with another one.

Debugging

We have all undoubtedly made so many mistakes while developing applications and spent a lot more hours trying to figure out what went wrong. Usually, it was just the small silly things, such as misplaced quotes or brackets, mistyped JSON, misspelled method names, overwritten global names (this one I did more than I do now, this is really a common problem when someone is asking for my help), and not installing the plugin at all or trying to use events for that plugin before PhoneGap has been initiated.

The debugging support for your PhoneGap application is not as good as it is for native applications or desktop web applications. The main obstacle is to be able to debug your browser on your mobile device, emulator, or Apache Ripple. This makes it difficult to synchronize the breakpoints or retrieve stack traces. However, we still have some options to go over that can be useful.

As we are developing for multiple platforms at the same time, there are not that many universal solutions that would work for all of the platforms simultaneously. Let's go over the different options that we have for debugging. Personally, I use a mixture of different approaches depending on what stage the application development is at and whether there is a need for accessing native APIs. So a majority of the debugging can be done in a regular web browser.

Desktop browsers

Desktop browsers are great and powerful tool for mobile web development and the best thing with them is that a majority of the mobile development can be tested in your desktop browser itself. They use the best built-in debugging support that you already use for web development in case you are a web developer. There are a few disadvantages of using this solution. There could be inconsistencies with the rendering accuracy due to different rendering engines on different mobile devices. As a computer is more powerful while processing heavy JavaScript, the code can be easily run and the last thing is the lack of native APIs on the computer. However, there are some solutions to partially overcome this.

When it comes to the selection of a desktop browser, it doesn't mean that you will be able to use the same browser as you use in your device, but a close alternative desktop browser that uses a similar browser rendering engine. The following table shows which desktop browsers can be used to emulate similar behavior as the mobile browser has:

Mobile Platform	Mobile Browser Engine	Compatible Desktop Browsers
Android	WebKit	Apple Safari, Google Chrome
Bada	WebKit	Apple Safari, Google Chrome

Mobile Platform	Mobile Browser Engine	Compatible Desktop Browsers
BlackBerry 5.0	Proprietary	None
BlackBerry 6.0+	WebKit	Apple Safari, Google Chrome
iOS	WebKit	Apple Safari, Google Chrome
Windows Phone	Internet Explorer	Internet Explorer

Basically, you have three options to go with: Google Chrome, Apple Safari, and Internet Explorer. As Google Chrome is the only one that is available for all the operating systems, I would recommend that you go with it. In my opinion, it has the best debugging tools for web development so far. If you plan to deploy your application to a Windows Phone, I would recommend that you perform another run on Internet Explorer to make sure that there are no inconsistencies, as the Internet Explorer rendering engine has its own peculiarities. So, in this book, all the instructions about how to use browsers are related to Google Chrome.

First thing that you need to do is to adjust the screen viewport to the mobile screen size in order to mimic the resolution. Chrome has a device mode `https://developer.chrome.com/devtools/docs/device-mode#enable-device-mode` in which you can easily do this and it already has predefined profiles for most of the popular mobile devices. Another great feature is that, in the device mode, you can do network throttling in order to simulate the internet connection speed on your mobile and you can see how it behaves.

In Google Chrome, you can also emulate the touch events `https://developer.chrome.com/devtools/docs/device-mode#device-sensors` that are otherwise not available on desktop browsers.

Now, when we have set up everything that we need to mimic the mobile device, we can use the debugging tools through a WebInspector to inspect the DOM and debug the JavaScript code.

The PhoneGap emulator

The PhoneGap emulator (`http://emulate.phonegap.com/`) is a desktop-based emulator for PhoneGap applications. Basically, it lets you run a PhoneGap application in your desktop application and simulates the various PhoneGap features that are not available on your computer. It has support for the main sensors that every mobile device has such as an accelerometer or geolocation. It simulates the camera API as well so that you can test application features that require camera input.

Weinre

Weinre (`http://people.apache.org/~pmuellr/weinre/docs/latest/`) is a tool that creates a local server that can communicate with a remote debug client for PhoneGap applications. It is quite simple to use. After installing and starting it up, you just need to add a few lines of code to your application and then restart it. Then you can open the development tool panel on your desktop in order to work with the application. The major advantage of Weinre is not that it competes with specific platform remote debugging, but that it supports a greater selection of operating systems and platforms than any other tool. Unfortunately, there are no breakpoints or stack traces available but JavaScript can give hints about errors.

When using the PhoneGap Build app, you don't need to install anything else because Weinre-based debugging is available right in the app screen in PhoneGap Build.

iOS Debugging

There are two sides of iOS debugging for the PhoneGap applications. For the iOS native side, you can use Xcode and for the web part, you can use Safari Remote Debugging.

Xcode

Xcode is a great IDE tool to develop native iOS applications and it has good debugging tools. Unfortunately it works only with the native code. However, you can use Xcode to debug the PhoneGap applications and therefore you will see if there are any errors or warnings coming from the application such as warnings that some of the plugins are missing. Every log output from the PhoneGap application can be seen in the debug area. Once you check that the main application is running properly on the simulator or the real device, you can switch to the next step that has been described next. Keep in mind that Xcode is meant to debug only the native code part; everything else is written in the JavaScript and thus not debuggable with Xcode, including the code inside the PhoneGap app.

Safari Remote Debugging

Safari has a great Web Inspector for web pages and, after iOS 6, it allows you to debug the web views in the native applications with the debugger for JS code. It uses Safari to connect to your device or the simulator and will connect the browser's development tools to the PhoneGap application. You will be able to use all the tools while you work on your desktop web application. You can set breakpoints in the JavaScript code and view the state of variables at the same time. Any warning or error will be printed in the console. You can also run commands in the console while your app is running. For more details about the setup, you can refer to the following link: `http://moduscreate.com/enable-remote-web-inspector-in-ios-6/`.

Android debugging

There is a solution for Android devices that is similar to the Safari Remote Debugging; however, this can be done from any desktop operating system. There are some limitations on the devices you can use, so the Android 4.4 (KitKat) with a minimum API level 19 and a Google Chrome desktop version higher than 32. You can read in detail about how to set up the working configurations from Chrome Documentation at `https://developer.chrome.com/devtools/docs/remote-debugging`. Once you connect your device through USB, you will be able to open the Web Inspector and use it in the same way as you would do with the web pages in the desktop Google Chrome. There are additional features that you can use such as the mirror option that shows your screen from the mobile device. There are many nice features added to it such as scrolling and clicking from the development tools, and it will update the actual mobile device.

User interface

PhoneGap is UI-agnostic by default. You can start from scratch with a plain HTML file and no CSS classes. This means that you can choose anything that you prefer. However, it is also a problem which one to choose, as there are many options such as choosing a unified look for all of the platforms or to go with a specific UI look and feel for every platform. We will go over some of the most popular choices, as follows:

- jQuery Mobile (`http://jquerymobile.com/`) is built on the jQuery UI foundation. jQuery Mobile is an HTML5-based user interface system designed to make responsive web sites and apps that are accessible on all smartphones, tablets, and desktop devices. The default UI look and feel resembles the jQuery UI, but extensive support with a wide array of themes can help you to quickly customize the default look and feel. Compared to some other frameworks described here, it just takes care of the UI part and you can use it with the other frameworks for the business logic. It is completely free for anyone to use.

- Twitter Bootstrap (http://getbootstrap.com/) is a free and open source collection of tools to create websites and web applications. It contains the HTML and CSS-based design templates for the typography, forms, buttons, navigation, and other interface components, as well as the optional JavaScript extensions. It aims to ease the development of dynamic websites and web applications. It is completely free for anyone to use.

- Ionic framework (http://ionicframework.com/) is a relatively new UI framework that is showing a lot of promise for the future, as it is a full single-page application framework. It is built on top of the AngularJS framework and so it imposes the development workflow and not just the UI. The good thing is that there are many libraries that are compatible with out-of-the-box. Even the main PhoneGap file that initiates the loading of the PhoneGap events and plugins is rewritten in order to work with the AngularJS dependency injection as a service provider. It is completely free for anyone to use.

- The Kendo UI (http://www.kendoui.com/) framework has emerged as a powerful and performance-minded framework for the mobile, web, and hybrid mobile applications. Kendo UI mobile provides both the UI widget and app framework functionality. It has support for the themes that give a native look and feel for every major mobile platform. Kendo UI is a paid framework, compared to others that are open sourced and free.

- Sencha Touch (https://www.sencha.com/products/touch/) is a mobile-focused HTML5 development platform that goes further than just providing only widget-focused features. It leans more to a full application framework and it provides its own MVC style architecture, complete with the storage, device profile, and top level abstractions. Sencha Touch is a commercial product.

- Ratchet (http://goratchet.com/) is a UI library that has its background in the Bootstrap UI library for desktop web applications. It was built on purpose to work well with all the mobile devices and has a more neutral UI look and feel for the applications. It is completely free for anyone to use.

- Topcoat Touch (http://www.agingcoder.com/topcoat-touch/) is a lean mobile framework that was designed from the ground up to build mobile apps on PhoneGap; as it is lightweight, it gives great performance results. It is a CSS-only framework and it doesn't impose on how you should work with your code. It is completely free for anyone to use.

- OnsenUI (http://onsen.io/) is a JavaScript and CSS framework for HTML5 web applications. It has a large selection of web-based UI components with responsive layout support. It is inspired by web components and so it is easy to build screens without the need of adding a lot of code. It works well with jQuery and AngularJS.

- ReactJS (`http://facebook.github.io/react/`) is technically not a UI framework on how to build a mobile application UI, but it is a whole new approach on how to build modular views for the single-page applications that have a fast response to data changes. It uses web components to render views and it is best when used with another CSS-only framework. Recently, React Native has been launched that will be doing all the code in JavaScript and HTML but still compile as a native application with native animations between the screens. It is completely free for anyone to use.

There is no shortage of choices when you need to build a user interface that fits with all mobile devices, but it is good if you think about the end user experience and what the users expect from the platform. Users of a specific platform are used to different workflows so the same user experience might not fit for all of them. The early mobile UI frameworks mimicked an iOS-style UI, but with the rise of Android devices that wasn't a viable option.

Besides the end user experience, there are some limitations imposed by the app stores themselves on which elements are encouraged or discouraged for use. You can read more about the guidelines for Human interface on different platforms at the following links:

- **iOS**: `https://developer.apple.com/library/ios/documentation/userexperience/conceptual/MobileHIG/index.html`
- **Android**: `https://developer.android.com/design/index.html`
- **Windows Phone**: `https://dev.windows.com/en-us/design`

Summary

In this chapter, we dived a bit into the more advanced topics that any PhoneGap developer should get into more detail once he/she has mastered the essential topics that we covered previously in this book. We went over the reasons why you should always test natively if it is possible, and found that debugging is not as straightforward as it is with a web inspector in the browser. We got to know about the UI frameworks that are available and specially built for mobile screens and learned some useful tips as well.

Index

Splashscreen plugin 66
StatusBar plugin
  about 67
  properties 82
Sublime Text 3
  URL 7
supported platforms, PhoneGap
  about 31, 32
  URL, for updates 31

T

template
  blank template 45
  hello-world template 45
  used, for creating Hello project 45
testing 140, 141
Titanium
  advantages 6
  disadvantages 6
  URL 6
Tizen
  URL 3
Topcoat Touch
  about 146
  URL 146
Twitter Bootstrap
  about 146
  URL 146

U

user interface
  about 145
  Ionic framework 146
  jQuery Mobile 145
  Kendo UI 146
  OnsenUI 146
  Ratchet 146
  ReactJS 147
  Sencha Touch 146
  Topcoat Touch 146
  Twitter Bootstrap 146

V

Vibration plugin
  about 67, 108, 109
  Vibrate method 109
  vibrating sequence, example 109, 110
  vibration, cancelling 110

W

web project development workflow 136
Weinre
  about 144
  URL 144

X

Xcode 144

Thank you for buying
PhoneGap Essentials

About Packt Publishing

Packt, pronounced 'packed', published its first book, *Mastering phpMyAdmin for Effective MySQL Management*, in April 2004, and subsequently continued to specialize in publishing highly focused books on specific technologies and solutions.

Our books and publications share the experiences of your fellow IT professionals in adapting and customizing today's systems, applications, and frameworks. Our solution-based books give you the knowledge and power to customize the software and technologies you're using to get the job done. Packt books are more specific and less general than the IT books you have seen in the past. Our unique business model allows us to bring you more focused information, giving you more of what you need to know, and less of what you don't.

Packt is a modern yet unique publishing company that focuses on producing quality, cutting-edge books for communities of developers, administrators, and newbies alike. For more information, please visit our website at www.packtpub.com.

About Packt Open Source

In 2010, Packt launched two new brands, Packt Open Source and Packt Enterprise, in order to continue its focus on specialization. This book is part of the Packt Open Source brand, home to books published on software built around open source licenses, and offering information to anybody from advanced developers to budding web designers. The Open Source brand also runs Packt's Open Source Royalty Scheme, by which Packt gives a royalty to each open source project about whose software a book is sold.

Writing for Packt

We welcome all inquiries from people who are interested in authoring. Book proposals should be sent to author@packtpub.com. If your book idea is still at an early stage and you would like to discuss it first before writing a formal book proposal, then please contact us; one of our commissioning editors will get in touch with you.

We're not just looking for published authors; if you have strong technical skills but no writing experience, our experienced editors can help you develop a writing career, or simply get some additional reward for your expertise.

PhoneGap 3.x Mobile Application Development HOTSHOT

ISBN: 978-1-78328-792-5   Paperback: 450 pages

Create useful and exciting real-world apps for iOS and Android devices with 12 fantastic projects

1. Use PhoneGap 3.x effectively to build real, functional mobile apps ranging from productivity apps to a simple arcade game.

2. Explore often-used design patterns in apps designed for mobile devices.

3. Fully practical, project-based approach to give you the confidence in developing your app independently.

PhoneGap 3 Beginner's Guide

ISBN: 978-1-78216-098-4   Paperback: 308 pages

A guide to building cross-platform apps using the W3C standards-based Cordova/PhoneGap framework

1. Understand the fundamentals of cross-platform mobile application development from build to distribution.

2. Learn to implement the most common features of modern mobile applications.

3. Take advantage of native mobile device capabilities—including the camera, geolocation, and local storage—using HTML, CSS, and JavaScript.

Please check **www.PacktPub.com** for information on our titles

PhoneGap Beginner's Guide

ISBN: 978-1-84951-536-8   Paperback: 328 pages

Build cross-platform mobile applications with the PhoneGap open source development framework

1. Learn how to use the PhoneGap mobile application framework.

2. Develop cross-platform code for iOS, Android, BlackBerry, and more.

3. Write robust and extensible JavaScript code.

4. Master new HTML5 and CSS3 APIs.

PhoneGap Mobile Application Development Cookbook

ISBN: 978-1-84951-858-1   Paperback: 320 pages

Over 40 recipes to create mobile applications using the PhoneGap API with examples and clear instructions

1. Use the PhoneGap API to create native mobile applications that work on a wide range of mobile devices.

2. Discover the native device features and functions you can access and include within your applications.

3. Packed with clear and concise examples to show you how to easily build native mobile applications.

Please check **www.PacktPub.com** for information on our titles